BAMBA BUTTERFLY

BY LEAD-IN LADY

© Lead-In Lady 2024

BAMBA BUTTERFLY

Published by Lead-In Lady

Johannesburg, South Africa

leadinlady100@gmail.com

2 4 6 8 10 9 7 5 3 1

Layout and cover design by Boutique Books

*In honour of those who display
hope in the midst of trials*

PROLOGUE - BAMBA BUTTERFLY

Beautiful beginnings do not signify beautiful endings in the same way that difficult beginnings do not signify difficult endings. We rise and fall throughout the course of life, and it is for us to find it within ourselves to face the world with a warm smile and a gentle heart. Forgiveness is the liberator of the soul. Learn to hold on to hope, which is present even in the darkest of times. Know that you have the ability to transform and that there are always butterflies (hope) around you. Bamba Butterfly.

CRIMSON STREAMS OF BLOOD FLOWED at a steady pace through makeshift gutters, in sharp contrast to the tan sand that was typical of Aguutar. The only sound present within the walls of the home was that of a red-faced, newly born child, who whimpered continuously. The others remained silent in the acceptance of impending death. The child, who had been wrenched from the safety of his mother's womb, was wrapped in a cotton cloth and returned to his young mother's arms as she continued to breathe the final breaths of her 17-year life. Her pain had numbed her, her blood loss had sent her into an unearthly paradigm, but the love of a mother for her child triumphed, and she held her son close with a faint smile on her lips and a softness in her glassy hazel eyes.

His whimpering settled and he opened his eyes to look silently at the most beautiful face that he would ever see. Her raven hair was spread across the bed, her fair skin glowed and the slight blush of her cheeks spoke of a woman very graceful and beautiful. Her face alone did not tell of the trauma that her body had experienced and, more importantly, the betrayal of her blood that flowed slowly but mercilessly out of its casing.

Her eyes closed and the wailing of her son resumed. These were the wails of a loss that he himself had no capacity to understand until later in life.

Silent tears washed down the faces of her mother and younger sister as they realised that they would need to, for the years to come, comfort the child as he had had at his disposal the physical care of his mother for under a few hours. The sheets, drenched in blood, were removed soon after the body of a young, meticulous and kind being was lifted for the compulsory bath that follows the death of a Muslim.

Shock reverberated through her mother, a soft-spoken and morally grounded woman who had faced so many difficulties in her own right. She had attended to the physical raising of her two precious daughters, who were three years apart, whilst her husband had been building a life in Africa.

It was common for men in the state of Aguutar to venture into Africa to build a business and subsequently build a future. It was also common for men to marry again in Africa, as had happened in this case, whilst first wives were left to tend to the lands back home. The love of a parent for his children probably does not diminish, even with the addition of sons and daughters in a new marriage, but active involvement in the life of children is something that cannot be compensated for.

For Khadeejah and Aaminah, the only influence they had in their life was through their mother, Halimah, who had instilled in them the qualities of kindness, the love of Allah and the importance of being a contributing member to society. Halimah did not have excessive resources, but adult neighbours and friends spent afternoons under the canopy of her front porch and stairs, where Halimah served warm rotis and freshly brewed tea whilst children played cricket on the sandy pathways.

KHADEEJAH, ACKNOWLEDGED FOR BOTH HER beauty and gentle character, had married at the age of 16 into a wealthy and well-respected family in Aguutar. Her marriage was widely celebrated in the village, but it was a marriage not destined to continue beyond the birth of their son, a mere year later. It was commonplace for women in the village to wilfully marry young and have children, but the lack of access to medical facilities placed these women at risk, especially when pregnancies steered out of the ordinary.

Both the doctor, who was a balding man who had arrived in a wagon, and the ageing nurse had tried to save the life of both child and mother, but with limited supplies and equipment the Rh incompatibility was a colossal impediment that caused a river of blood too wide to cross.

It is, perhaps a miracle that it was the mother who'd passed and the new life that blossomed, as it was accepted that Rh incompatibility would result in a child being stillborn or, at best, being anaemic. Miracles, however, sometimes happen so that other miracles can occur later in life. There is, of course, a purpose that every being must fulfil before leaving the world. The Moulana, who had performed the beautiful act of reciting the azaan into the ears of the newborn, carried the duty of performing the *janaazah salaah* at the funeral of the newborn's mother, and this could serve only as an example of how life and death are so intricately entwined. Pieces of humans can continue to live whilst they themselves do not. Children are, after all, a living legacy.

The villagers, who had enjoyed the loving and kind nature of Khadeejah, were distraught at the news of this tragedy, but the news of her death and the birth of her son was yet to be communicated to her husband, who was on a trip to a village a few hours away. News reached him days later and, if there had been any grief, it was concealed as he continued with his daily activities. His son remained in the care of his grandmother and aunt, who vehemently protected his interests.

Halimah, overcome by grief, would lie restlessly on the marble floor, night after night, not resting but yearning only to see her child. The baby grappled to settle, and mountainous medical bills accumulated as Halimah and Aaminah searched for the reason why the child brought up his milk. He didn't gain weight easily and portions of milk consumed would be brought up soon after. The child suffered from what appeared to be reflux, but the village did not have any remedy available. The rusty, poorly built doctor's wagon became a standard feature outside their home as they battled to find a source of nourishment for the sickly child.

Grief has no cure but time and it was with time that the wide-eyed child settled and grew finding comfort in a red sheet that he carried around the house and on every excursion that he went on. The child, no doubt, had recognised the comfort that he had felt in the arms of his own mother as they lay on blood-drenched sheets and for that reason became attached to a red sheet that consoled him.

His aunt maintained her vibrancy and her willingness to bring light into this tormented home and she dressed her nephew in a pair of dungarees and allowed the village photographer to picture her with her beloved as he sat in her arms, distracted momentarily by the gleam of her lengthy gold earrings. She kept the picture tucked away safely in a satin pouch. Her sister would have been so proud of her little boy. His wide forehead, rounded eyes and height made him stand out amongst children his age and he spoke his first words in a sweetness remarkably close to his mother's voice. His aunt cajoled him into having his milk, consulted lengthily with doctors, and communicated with him not only in their mother-tongue but in the language of a pure and undivided love that matched only the love that his grandmother had for him.

Hawa's tears combined with the water in the enamel bath where she bathed her daughter. Hawa had heard the news of the death of her childhood friend, Khadeejah. Hawa had last seen Khadeejah in Aguutar over a decade ago, but she had always earnestly awaited her letters. She had been heartbroken when Aaminah responded to her last letter with the news that Khadeejah had passed away giving birth to a son. Khadeejah's death was a mere six months before Hawa gave birth to her own daughter, her third child, in South Africa. Hawa had not known about her friend's passing.

Hawa, a gentle-faced woman with hazel eyes and dark hair, had been blessed with three beautiful children before the age of 20. Her father had abandoned her and her mother within days of her birth, and he had left for South Africa, leaving them to fend for themselves. He had married again and started his own family, like so many other men, but he differed in as much as he'd divorced his wife. This was something unheard of in Aguutar but, left destitute, Hawa's mother remarried as a second wife and left Hawa in the care of her uncle.

Hawa was a gentle being who didn't harden with the tribulations that life had offered her, and she accompanied her uncle when he left for South Africa. It was in South Africa that her marriage to Rashid was arranged. He was a young man who had squandered his inheritance, but as a girl from a poor background she wasn't given much of an option despite her beauty and excellent character. She married young and had a son and two daughters.

Hawa placed her rosy-cheeked daughter into a cloth cradle (*jhoola*) and then walked into the adjacent kitchen. The kitchen comprised a wooden unit, a square table and a coal stove. She put the two remaining slices of bread onto two blue enamel plates and set it on the table. She seated her four-year-old son and two-year-old daughter at the table. They were beautiful, gold-haired children, but they had not been given the opportunity to put on any form of baby fat. They ate their supper slowly and Hawa saw the exhaustion in their sunken eyes.

She wiped their faces after supper and sent them to bed. They shared a single bed next to Hawa's and in minutes they were asleep. Hawa and Rashid would not eat again tonight. This was the third consecutive day of no food. Hawa drank some water and checked on Salma, her beautiful baby.

"One day you shall marry the son of my friend," she promised.

RASHID HANDED HIS LAST BUNCH of flowers to a man in a cream vehicle. The man grabbed the flowers and flung payment at Rashid. Rashid was accustomed to this type of behaviour; this was, after all, apartheid South Africa, and all that he was really concerned with was making enough money from the sale of his bunches of flowers to pay the rental and buy his family some food.

Rashid dabbed at the sweat that had accumulated on his forehead as he began to walk away from the last set of traffic lights outside the General Hospital in Johannesburg towards the train station. It was before dusk that he reached Kliptown, but the stores were already closed. There would be no supper again tonight. Hawa heard the door close and lowered her gaze immediately when she saw that Rashid had come home empty-handed. She didn't wish to make him feel inadequate.

"Shops were closed. We will buy something tomorrow. I was late," he informed her.

"It's okay," Hawa said, managing a smile.

The children had gone to bed already and within minutes Hawa and Rashid slipped into a hunger-driven sleep.

A knock at the door interrupted the family's breakfast. Rashid had risen early to buy some groceries. He'd also made his weekly contribution to the landlord. Rashid generally made more money on a Friday, as on other days he managed to sell two bunches of flowers at best. He would use that money to purchase bread and eggs for his family during the week, but there were many days when he and Hawa would go to bed hungry because they kept the bread and eggs for the children.

"*Assalaamu alaikum,*" the neighbour, Saleha said, as she entered the house.

Saleha was a dressmaker who lived across the street. Saleha and her husband loved children and admired Hawa and Rashid's very beautiful offspring.

"*Wa alaykum salaam,*" Hawa responded.

"Please join us," Rashid offered, beckoning towards the table.

"Thank you. Perhaps next time. I sewed Salma a dress. May I take her to try it on?" Saleha asked.

Hawa nodded and Saleha lifted the smiling child from her cloth cradle.

Tears brimmed in Hawa's eyes. "Thank you," Hawa said to Saleha, overcome with emotion.

Saleha's heart broke.

Salma's clothes were hand-me-downs and none of them fit her. This would be the first time that she would have something her size. Hawa was so grateful.

Rashid left for work within the next few minutes, and he reminded Hawa to pack before leaving. Hawa and the children would be leaving for Bertrams on Monday. Hawa's aunt lived in Bertrams, and a driver was sent every second month to collect her and the children. They would spend a week there before returning home. It was a huge relief that for a week the children would be well-fed, but Hawa always felt that she would never be able to repay the family for their kindness. She felt like a burden, even though she wasn't received as one. Hawa cleared breakfast as her son and daughter rolled a rag-made ball across the floor. She had lost all hope for herself, and her only wish was that her children would find ease.

HALIMAH DREW HER BREATH IN as Imtiyaaz tugged on her green punjabi.

"Maaaama. Maamaaaa. Mam. A. Mama," he said.

She looked into his wide eyes and lifted her grandson up from the floor. Halimah was setting the table as her son-in-law was due to visit with his father, Omar. Omar was visiting from South Africa, having settled there many years ago. Omar's first wife was from a powerful and well-respected family in Aguutar and, even though she was a kind woman, she had insisted on settling in South Africa with Omar to the exclusion of his second wife, who had borne four children. His second marriage had been concluded for the sole purpose of having children as his wife was unable to conceive.

Omar saw his second wife occasionally when he visited Aguutar. On this trip he would be taking his children with him to South Africa, where they would permanently reside. He didn't plan on returning for several years. Umayma, his second wife, would be left to tend to the lands. She would, for all intents and purposes, be left alone and the thought of not seeing her children devastated her. She had been advised that this was the way of the world and she had been told to accept that humble beginnings determined the course of her life. Umayma visited her grandson daily and she cherished her time with him, but she knew in the depths of her heart that her son would claim his own son eventually, in the same way that Omar had claimed their children to her exclusion.

Halimah hadn't seen much of Imtiyaaz's father, Hoosen, since his wife's death, but she had come to know that he was keen to move on with a new life. Umayma had informed her that Hoosen would be settling in South Africa along with his three sisters: the latter being 15, 13 and 11 respectively. Halimah's heart had been shattered when she had heard this news as she acknowledged the impact this would have on Umayma.

Pleasantries were exchanged and Omar clutched on to his grandson. This was their first meeting. His grandson settled into his arms without much ado and stayed there for the duration of the meal. Hoosen barely acknowledged his son and didn't do much more than enquire after his health. Soon after lunch, Omar announced that he would be departing from Aguutar with his children at the close of six weeks. He stated firmly that he would be taking Imtiyaaz to stay with him and Umayma the following week, as he wished to spend time with his grandchild.

"Thank you for looking after my heir, Halimah. It's important that Hoosen settles in South Africa. He needs to take the business over from me and then it will pass to Imtiyaaz," he stated.

Halimah dropped her gaze.

"Halimah. You do know that the boy will only be with you until the age of seven. I will someday be collecting him from you," Omar said as he and Hoosen prepared to leave.

Halimah sank to the floor and her tears formed puddles around her. Her grandson, her life, and her link to Khadeejah, would be taken away from her. Imtiyaaz, sensing her pain, began to cry as he tried to seek comfort in her. She enveloped him in her arms and their tears flowed as one stream.

Halimah carefully folded items of clothing before packing them into a brown leather bag.

"Don't worry, Ma. It's just a few days," Aaminah said, holding back tears.

"For now," Halimah answered.

"If they take him away to Africa, we will go too," Aaminah said, trying to sound convincing.

"How so? Papa has a new family. We have to stay here and look after the properties. The land," Halimah said quietly.

"Why can't Papa get someone to help? Why must we live like this? In constant sadness? My sister left this world and now we must accept that our boy will be taken to some country that we have only heard about. Whilst we stay here!" Aaminah cried.

Halimah stared blankly at her daughter. Halimah regretted bringing the issue up, but she was overcome with an impending sense of doom. Children grew fast; the rains would be starting soon, and it would be only a matter of time before they parted with Imtiyaaz.

"Hush my child. This is a problem of the future. You will be married by then. Who knows? You may marry in Africa and then you will see to the light of my life," Halimah stated, wiping her own tears.

"Sister Halimah, are you here?" a female voice called out.

"Jee, who is it?" Halimah answered, noting immediately from the dialect that it was a woman who probably held the role of a servant.

"Omar Bhai wanted me to bring these," the tall woman with a neat plait informed her, gesturing to an array of items on the floor.

"These are gifts from brother in Africa," the woman continued, excitedly.

Halimah nodded. She recognised the handwriting on an envelope perched on a box. Her husband had remembered them. Halimah smiled, clutching at the gold locket he had gifted her two weeks into their marriage.

"Does my Papa think sending gifts will replace his presence?" Aaminah asked, the sadness evident in her voice.

"Don't think of it that way, child," Omar said, as he stepped into the house.

Aaminah immediately lowered her gaze.

"Aaminah speaks with a childish longing," Halimah explained.

Omar nodded. "He sent all these parcels with me, but I didn't have the chance to unpack before our first meeting," Omar explained.

"It's no worry," Halimah answered.

"My grandson?" Omar asked, his eyes scanning the room.

"Aaminah, please bring Imtiyaaz down," Halimah said, her voice shaking.

Aaminah returned with Imtiyaaz clutching her right hand. Halimah handed Safiyya, Omar's help, the bag.

"He will return next Thursday," Omar said, pulling Imtiyaaz towards him.

The threesome set out towards their family home and Omar couldn't help but compare Aguutar to South Africa. He had grown up in Aguutar and had enjoyed the afternoon teas with freshly made rotis and the aroma of spices in the market. He didn't miss tending to the livestock or being dependent on the fruits of the land, though. He far preferred owning a shop in South Africa, where he could trade, albeit with limitations imposed by white rule.

Omar looked down at his grandson. He had silky hair that shone in the sunlight. He seemed delighted to be outside. His grandson was a fragile creature who beamed at all those who looked in his direction. A gentle heart in a tough world.

HALIMAH DRAPED HER MINT SCARF loosely around her head and stepped onto her veranda. Her bangles clamoured as she rocked on a swing, considering the way in which the streaks of sunlight caused the leaves of her plants to glisten. She had long forgotten what fresh air smelt like as the air in Aguutar spoke of overpopulation and poor sewerage systems.

She opened the manila envelope, careful not to rip it. Her eyes settled on her husband's neat hand.

Halimah,

My heart has not witnessed a greater pain than knowing that we have lost our daughter. The birth of a child is generally a time of immense joy, but for us it has signified a time of overpowering sadness. I am grateful that you and Aaminah are there to care for our grandchild and I ask that you assist me in doing all that is possible for him to never feel that something is lacking in his life.

I received word that he is a sickly child with different forms of milk not agreeing with him. I have purchased a fridge, and it will be arriving at Port Perowree in the following weeks. I am hoping that perhaps if his milk is kept at the right temperature that would assist. I was given that advice from a family friend who has studied medicine. It does require an electrical connection, so I have asked Omar Bhai to assist with seeing to that whilst he is in Aguvtar. Fridges are quite useful; I have both a fridge and freezer here in South Africa and I couldn't help but think of you.

Yasmeen has given birth to another daughter; I have four other children now. You will meet them someday. I just haven't been able to come to Aguvtar. I am establishing businesses in South Africa. Amin Bhai, my younger cousin, is running the one shop but I have bought another, and I am looking into opening a wholesale business. I will be moving to central Johannesburg soon. There aren't many Indian people in that area, but I have received a concession. It has something to do with my finances. The government has many rules, but I have seen that there are many exceptions.

I hope that you and Aaminah like the gifts. Yasmeen knitted a blanket for Imtiyaaz. She sends her salaams.

I will write to you again. There is also some money in this envelope. I hope it helps you.

Greetings and duas to all family and neighbours

Halimah placed the letter at her side. His letter was factual but lacked any outright display of love for her and Aaminah. She knew about his family, and she appreciated that he had reached out to her, but she couldn't shake the feeling of sadness in knowing that he had his own family unit, which excluded her. She was not averse to him having a second wife, and she had heard that Yasmeen was a kind woman. All she sought was recognition as well. Halimah had given up her whole life for someone who belonged to someone else. She thought of the wave of happiness she'd experienced the day before, when she had received the parcels and letter. She had foolishly been hoping that in remembering them, he would offer some form of emotional support. She would, however, be left in constant wanting.

Hawa smiled as she dished out some chicken curry and rice. A compassionate woman, Shameema Patel, had asked Hawa to assist her with running her home industry.

Shameema made and sold *papadums* and the demand for these had significantly increased over the past few months. Shameema could afford to hire help, but she had asked Hawa to assist her four days a week in exchange for providing the family with a meal on each day that Hawa worked there. Shameema understood that Rashid would not have allowed Hawa to work for monetary payment, but Shameema and her husband had noted that the children looked malnourished and saw this as an opportunity to help Hawa without infringing upon her dignity. Shameema admired Hawa's jovial spirit. She had been dealt multiple blows but her *sabr* was noteworthy. It is not often that women so pure walk this earth.

Hawa put the only two dishing out bowls she owned on the white panelite table. She had eaten lunch with the children at the Patel's household and they had sent a meal for Rashid as they did each time that she went to assist with making *papadums*. Rashid ate gratefully but he couldn't dispense with the feeling that he had let his family down.

Rashid had moved to South Africa as a 10-year-old, and he had witnessed the death of his father a mere year later. Rashid had returned to Aguutar to live with his mother. He had begun to run through his father's wealth, and as an only child his mother had indulged him. He had returned to South Africa at the point when all that remained was the stretch of land near the railway that they owned in Aguutar, along with their house. He knew that the land had great value but, realising that he had spent a large segment of his inheritance, he opted to work for a living.

Within two years of working in South Africa his mother had passed away and he lost his bearing. He married Hawa and had children, but when he'd attempted to sell his land and bring the funds into South Africa, he had found that a family had settled on the land and had somehow assumed ownership. Rashid didn't have enough funds to dispute the land ownership and so he lost all that was once his. He received no support from the community as they feared the family who had usurped the land. Rashid joined the ranks of the poor and he vowed to work hard to provide for his family. He realised with time that, even though he worked hard, he couldn't provide fully, and this pained him greatly.

His children would need to school and he knew he needed to approach the local *Jamaat* for assistance. This too was a great source of shame; he feared that he had become a beggar.

The rains had come and gone twice, and Halimah pinned Aaminah's bridal veil. It was a deep turquoise with gold trimmings. Aaminah's anklets jingled as she turned to face a full-length mirror. Aaminah had opted to wear a turquoise bridal *salwar* as opposed to the more common red. Aaminah caught sight of the tears in her mother's eyes. Imtiyaaz sat quietly on the edge of the bed. He was dressed in a perfectly tailored grey suit, sent by his grandfather. Aaminah's father couldn't attend the wedding ceremony, but he had arranged for a week-long celebration. He had had three more children, a total of seven in South Africa, but she stood on her wedding day without the representation of a father or a sibling.

"Khala," Imtiyaaz said, breaking the silence.

"Jee, my child," Aaminah answered, turning to look at him.

"I like your dress. You look like an angel. Like every day. Are you an angel?" he questioned.

"Have you seen an angel before?" Aaminah asked.

"Aunty Fatima says angels are pretty and look after people. You are pretty and you look after me," Imtiyaaz said.

Aaminah and Halimah were lost for words. Imtiyaaz, even at such a tender age, spoke with a resounding wisdom.

"Well then, you must be an angel too," Aaminah said walking toward him and sitting on the edge of the bed. She clasped his hand in hers.

"Don't go! Don't leave me!" Imtiyaaz wailed.

Halimah, overcome with emotion, drew her beloved into her arms.

"I will never leave you," Aaminah sobbed. "I am going to live on the next street. I will be here for you every day," she promised.

Aaminah, despite the receipt of multiple proposals, had waited to accept one where it was acknowledged and understood that she was needed at home on an emotional level. Aaminah was a protected child, with Halimah seeing to all her needs, and assuming most of the household chores. Halimah had showered an infinite amount of love on her daughter and the three of them were inseparable. Imtiyaaz depended on both Halimah and Aaminah as he had from the second his mother had left the world.

Losses happen in life; but there are gains as well and Imtiyaaz had gained the immense love of both souls. A love that knew no bounds.

Halimah drew away from her daughter and grandson, dabbed at her eyes and excused herself.

"I'm going to check on whether all the *mithai* is laid-out," she said and headed out of the doorway.

An hour later, Aaminah and Imtiyaaz emerged, hand in hand. He was ready to give her away, in place of her father.

RASHID'S SHOULDERS DROOPED AS HE walked home carrying a box of unsold flowers. He had spent the entire day outside the hospital but hadn't been able to make any sales. His feet had developed blisters from pacing up and down.

"Rashid Bhai," a deep voice called out as he passed by the Khan household. Muqtaar Khan was seated on his veranda, sipping on tea.

"*Assalaamu alaikum*," Rashid answered, stopping at the freshly painted white gate.

"You were just the person I was waiting for! Please, come in. Mind the paint; wait, let me help," Muqtaar said as he quickly rose from his cane chair to let Rashid in.

Rashid, slightly baffled, followed Muqtaar onto the veranda.

"Zuleika! Please make a fresh pot of tea. Rashid Bhai is here," Muqtaar called out.

"Are those flowers going to be delivered?" Muqtaar asked, gesturing toward the box.

"No," Rashid answered, and Muqtaar responded with a grin. Muqtaar, jumping to his feet, exclaimed, "Rashid Bhai! You saved my life! It is my wedding anniversary! I didn't get her a gift, but she will forgive me when she sees that I have arranged for a box of flowers." Muqtaar pulled a note out of his wallet.

"I, uh, I don't want payment. You can have the flowers. Happy anniversary!" Rashid replied, not accepting the note.

The value of the note far exceeded the worth of the flowers.

"Do not upset a neighbour!" Muqtaar warned.

Zuleika emerged from the house carrying a tray of tea, freshly fried samoosas, and a few slices of coconut cake.

Zuleika greeted Rashid and placed the tray on the table.

"Wife! Brother Rashid has delivered a box of flowers for you! Eight bunches! Happy anniversary!" Muqtaar said, winking at his wife.

Zuleika knew her husband well and immediately caught on. "Rashid Bhai! This is a wonderful surprise! Thank you for doing this!" Zuleika said, beaming.

Rashid smiled and said, "Happy anniversary, Sister."

Muqtaar sat back.

Zuleika excused herself and Muqtaar turned to Rashid. "A rep came by here yesterday. He mentioned a job for a retail manager in Middelburg. Give it some thought," Muqtaar said.

Rashid and Muqtaar discussed the opportunity and Rashid returned home that evening with more money than anticipated and the hope of a new job.

Pools of blood surrounded Aaminah. She screamed in pain as her child was ripped from her. Halimah watched in horror as life escaped the body of both mother and child.

Halimah awoke with a start, gasping for breath. She looked around the room and saw Imtiyaaz sleeping soundly next to her. Halimah walked over to the clay pot filled with water. She poured some into her palms and passed it over her face. Halimah had been having nightmares about losing Aaminah in the same way that she had lost her eldest daughter.

Aaminah was approaching her third trimester and as each day passed, Halimah grew more and more anxious. Aaminah had been married for almost a year and it had warmed her heart to see how well her daughter was treated by both her husband and her mother-in-law. She was treasured and protected, and no objections were raised when Aaminah chose to spend the day in the company of Halimah and Imtiyaaz. The onset of her pregnancy, however, had been a huge cause of concern for Halimah, while Aaminah approached the upcoming birth with a sense of excitement and positivity.

"Ma. Mama," came Imtiyaaz's small voice.

Halimah, upset that she had woken him, answered, "Jee, my child?"

"Is it morning now?" he asked, rubbing his eyes.

"No, it isn't. Go back to sleep now," Halimah said, gently.

She stroked his forehead.

"Can we go to the market tomorrow? Khala promised," Imtiyaaz asked.

"Yes, we can," Halimah responded, smiling.

"If it is not morning, why are you awake?" Imtiyaaz, questioned.

"I, uh, I needed some water," Halimah answered.

"I heard Aunty Fatima say that Khala is due to have a baby. What does that mean?" Imtiyaaz asked.

Halimah was silent for a moment, unsure of how to answer. "It means that Khala is going to get a little boy or girl, like you, as a present," Halimah explained.

"Did my mommy get me as a present?" Imtiyaaz asked.

Halimah held back her tears, something she had had to learn to master. Imtiyaaz had learnt that his mom had passed away and had gone to live in a beautiful place. He had accepted the explanation given and had asked questions about why she'd left him, what she looked like, and whether she would send him letters the way Nana did.

"Yes, you are her biggest present," Halimah said.

"Is Khala going to live with her too? In that place with chocolate rivers? Is she going to leave us too?" Imtiyaaz asked, his voice trembling.

"No," Halimah said firmly.

"Why did my mommy go then? Is it some mommies and not others? I don't want Khala to go!" Imtiyaaz wailed.

Halimah found no answer and could give him nothing more than a reassuring hug.

HAWA GAZED AT THE CHILDREN who had dozed off on the back seat of the Patel's car. They were headed towards Middelburg, but dusk had fallen as Rashid had hired a van that was available only after 4PM at a nominal rate. It hadn't taken too long to load the van, as they had limited items. The Patel family had been kind enough to offer to drive the family up to Middelburg. Rashid was excited about the new beginning, and he had promised Hawa that he would put in every effort to provide fully. She had assured him that they would make do and that the most important thing was the well-being of the children.

The car arrived outside a house with a blue door. The house was on what appeared to be a main road and Rashid squinted as he double-checked the address.

"This is it," Rashid confirmed.

The van pulled over behind the car and the men got out. Rashid approached the house to the right and waited patiently for an answer to his knock. A beady eyed girl, nothing older than 12, answered the door.

"*Assalaamu alaikum.* I am so sorry to disturb you. I'm the neighbour. Do you p..." Rashid wasn't given the opportunity to finish his sentence as the girl turned away. She retrieved the key and handed it to him.

"My father isn't home yet. I will send him to your house when he arrives," she informed him matter-of-factly before pushing the door closed.

Rashid ran his hand over a wide crack on the front door and sighed as he pushed it open. He looked into an empty room with a steel basin in the corner and a coal stove on the opposite wall. The men followed him in. The house included an adjacent room which could be used as a separate bedroom and there was a tiny passageway which led to a bathroom of sorts. Broken cream tiles covered a quarter of the wall and a tap stood leaking in the right-hand corner.

"Let's try and fix that up," his soon-to-be ex-neighbour said.

"Yes. Let's. We can only try our best to fix all that is broken, one way or another," Rashid replied.

RASHID IGNORED THE DULL PAIN in his right foot. He had missed a step the previous day and had fallen onto the cement floor in the storeroom at work. It didn't really help that he had to be on his feet for 15-hour days with a day off every second week.

Rashid was committed to doing his best, but he had been slightly disappointed when his boss had only paid him half of his promised wage. His boss had offered no explanation and the following week, when he received half of his wage again, Rashid politely asked for the reason. His boss, a short man who wore black-rimmed glasses, had only then taken the liberty to advise him that the advertised wage was relevant only to peak season months. Rashid had stared blankly at the man and, even though he was grateful to be earning, he wasn't able to improve his family's life in any way.

"I see you have a limp," his boss, Mr Dhorat, commented.

"It's nothing," Rashid said, trying to stand a bit straighter.

"It'd better be nothing. You haven't been working here long and you already look sickly," Mr Dhorat commented.

Rashid felt his heart rate quicken. He needed this job.

"I really am fine," Rashid assured him.

"I'm going to Durban for a week" Mr Dhorat informed him. "My brother will be here to watch over you and the other staff."

Rashid nodded.

"Stop standing here and nodding at me! I need you to check on customers," Mr Dhorat barked.

Rashid, startled, walked away and clenched his teeth as he tried to disguise his limp.

Mr Dhorat's brother turned out to have a foul temper and Rashid found himself dreading work. He was beyond relieved that he had Sunday off this week and he and the staff waited patiently to receive their wages on Saturday evening.

"What are you people waiting for? Money? You do nothing the entire day, lazing around the whole week, and now you want money?" the foul-tempered man asked, scathingly.

The staff complement, which comprised four men and a middle-aged woman, remained silent. They had spent additional hours at work this week and had been verbally abused and shamed for no reason at all.

"No wages! Ungrateful and useless rats," he mocked, before ordering them to leave the shop.

Rashid, confused by this behaviour, turned to his colleague Afzal as soon as they reached the main road.

"Why didn't we get our wages?" Rashid asked.

"Oh, that's normal. Dhorat Junior normally takes and spends our wage money. You'll see. He comes to the shop for a week every month," Afzal explained.

"Why? That's wrong! What kind of treatment is this?" Rashid asked, the anger seeping through his voice.

"The treatment designed for the poor. Like us," Afzal replied.

Hawa and Rashid went hungry for the next few days and on the next Saturday, when Rashid received a quarter of his promised pay for no reason, he walked out of the shop never to return.

"Ah, we will all fit. Don't worry. These children are thin," Dimpho, an aging truck driver, assured Rashid.

Dimpho, who delivered paraffin, had agreed to assist Rashid and the family with transporting themselves and their items. There wasn't much seating in the truck, but Rashid had no other available means of going back to his old neighbourhood.

Hawa had explained to the children that they were going back home as Daddy had a better job offer back in their old neighbourhood. Hawa was worried about unsettling them as she had noticed that Hamza had come to the understanding that the family was facing a great amount of difficulty. He had become withdrawn and edgy and Hawa was worried about the psychological impact stemming from the instability.

Rashid lifted Salma into the truck. Salma's once rosy cheeks had disappeared into a paleness and the signs of malnourishment were glaring. The truck set off and the family headed east of Middelburg with Dimpho. They would have to follow his delivery route and would probably only reach the old neighbourhood in the evening. Rashid had sent word to the Patel family, who had immediately offered to host them until they found a new place to rent.

It was less than an hour later when the truck approached an agricultural holding of sorts. Dimpho completed a few deliveries in the area and moved along into the vicinity of Pan, adjacent to Arnot. The truck came to a halt outside a large farm-style house. A middle-aged woman, with sandy brown hair and creamy skin, sat on the *stoep*, enjoying the cool breeze.

"Hello, Dimpho. How are you?" she asked, as Dimpho placed two cans of paraffin near the front door.

"Okay and you, Mama?" Dimpho responded.

"Okay. You delivered earlier than usual," Zohra Bai commented.

"Yes. I am helping a man and his family move. It's such a shame. He left his job and doesn't have money for transport," Dimpho said.

Zohra Bai looked in the direction of the truck and her gaze fell on Salma. The little girl, whose cheeks were reddened from the sun, looked wide-eyed at Zohra. Zohra got up and walked towards the truck.

Zohra knocked at the passenger window and Hawa rolled it down.

"*Assalaamu alaikum,*" Zohra greeted.

Rashid and Hawa replied in unison.

"I hear that you are travelling because you lost your job," Zohra said. She was a direct woman, the wife of a wealthy businessman, and she had an overwhelming confidence.

"Jee," Rashid answered.

"My name is Zohra Mayet. I am married to Moosa Mayet, and we own this farm and the shop on it," she said, pointing to a green building in the distance.

"There's a vacancy at our shop. Our manager just left. You can offload your goods if you are interested in the job. My husband will be here after lunch. He had a court case to attend," Zohra said, barely stopping to breathe.

Rashid, quite taken aback by the direct approach of the woman, wasn't sure how to react. He was unsure of whether he should accept the offer from the woman, as surely it would need her husband's approval. It seemed almost unreal and following the last débâcle Rashid was sceptical. The woman had mentioned the husband was at a court case, and that wasn't a great indicator either.

Hawa cleared her throat and that broke the silence.

"You can discuss further with my husband. If he doesn't like you, you have my word that I will arrange transport for you tomorrow," Zohra said, her tone softening.

She realised from his expression that he was alarmed.

Zohra and her husband had been looking for a replacement manager for months but because of the distance from urban life they hadn't managed to secure one for more than two weeks at a time. This seemed to be a perfect opportunity for both them and Rashid.

Rashid wasn't sure what came over him, but he motioned for Hawa to open the door.

He had nothing, so he wasn't really in the position to lose any more.

IMTIYAAZ PULLED FACES AT A dark-eyed little girl who squealed with delight. She was seven months old and had found a companion in Imtiyaaz. It was not unusual for him to rush off after his breakfast to Aaminah's house, where he would spend the entire day with his baby cousin. Aaminah had given birth to a healthy little girl of three kilograms.

Halimah had recovered from her anxiety the minute she saw Aaminah with her granddaughter. Aaminah had initially feared that Imtiyaaz would withdraw on the birth of her child, so she had made every effort to include him. He had taken to having a baby around very well and, instead of being concerned about having to share the attention, he showered both Aaminah and baby Maryam with love.

It was after dusk on a Wednesday evening when Halimah heard a voice outside the front door. She was not accustomed to receiving guests at that hour, so she tied her scarf around her head and peered outside through a small gap. She saw a thin boy standing awkwardly at the door, clutching an envelope. Halimah opened the door wider, and the boy thrust the envelope into her hands before rushing down the stairs.

Halimah, slightly baffled, tore open the envelope and retrieved a letter, in her husband's hand.

Assalaamu alaikum, Halimah. Mubarak. I am so pleased to hear of the birth of my second grandchild. Our grandchild. I long to be in their presence and my deepest wish is to have them integrate with my children. Part of that wish of mine is to come true; word has it that the boy's father has found a potential wife. It would be likely that Imtiyaaz will move to South Africa within the space of a year, just so he settles in. I know that this may aggrieve you, but it is for the best. We must look at his future. Please gift Aaminah the cash in the envelope.

Greetings to all.

Halimah felt her chest tighten and she found herself gasping for air. The room swirled around her, and she held onto the banister for support. They had stayed true to their word. Her light was leaving. She took deep breaths; she couldn't let him know about her pain.

"Mama!" Imtiyaaz called.

Halimah held onto the sound of his voice; knowing she needed to memorise it.

"Milk time!" he announced as he stood in the hallway, dressed in his crisp white pyjamas.

Halimah managed a smile, gathered him in her arms, and walked into the kitchen. These were stolen moments that she would need to build a lifetime on.

HALIMAH PREPARED IMTIYAAZ'S FAVOURITE BREAKFAST comprising chocolate and coconut pancakes, *badaam* milk, and *puri*. Aaminah had slept over and they had both clung to Imtiyaaz. The day had come: he was leaving. Aaminah and Halimah had been admonished for treating his departure like a funeral, but in many ways it was. Halimah was losing her purpose; she would be left with nothing to do and no one to care for. Aaminah came home regularly to spend time with Halimah and Imtiyaaz, but as evening arrived she too would head back to her marital home.

Imtiyaaz arrived at the table, holding his red sheet. He had, over the past year, held on to his sheet less and less but he was drawing comfort from it now, knowing that his world was about to change.

"I don't want to go," Imtiyaaz squeaked.

"Mama's love. You have to go. Your papa is waiting. He has a big house and he bought you lots of toys. You are going to start school there. Learn new things; become a big businessman like your grandfather. You have to, right? You will have to grow up and then look after me. I'm going to visit. I'll be there in a few months," Halimah said.

She had rehearsed this time and time again. Her heart was broken but she needed to conceal it from him as it would disturb him hugely if he knew her pain.

"I like this house. I don't want toys. I want you," Imtiyaaz cried.

"Don't be silly! Behave now! Eat your food! Your grandfather is coming," Halimah said, forcing anger into her voice.

She turned away from him. Aaminah was less in control of her emotions. She sat motionless at the base of the staircase; her eyes puffy.

"Strength for and to him," Halimah whispered.

She wasn't sure if Aaminah heard as she remained in the same spot until Omar and Umayma arrived. Umayma would be accompanying them on the journey, but her pain was evident as well.

The family journeyed to Port Perowree, with Imtiyaaz gazing back longingly at his familiar surrounds. He drew his sheet closer to him and his love for his aunt and grandmother funded his tears. Halimah's eyes deadened as they took Imtiyaaz out of her arms. He screamed and kicked and that was the final vision she had of him as he was taken aboard.

"Rashid. I would like to get your permission for something," Hawa asked, as she kept her gaze lowered.

Rashid, who sat upright on a newly purchased couch, turned to Hawa and smiled. "What is it?" he responded.

"I have received word that my best friend's son, little Imtiyaaz, has moved to Joburg. I would like to see him, when you have some time off," Hawa said.

"Of course. I know how important Khadeejah was to you. It's no problem at all. I have a day off next Sunday," Rashid replied, "I will make arrangements with my boss to use his car."

"Thank you," Hawa said gratefully.

"With whom is he going to be living?" Rashid asked.

"With Khadeejah's father-in-law, Omar Bhai. Hoosen travels a lot, I think," Hawa answered.

"The tycoon himself," Rashid responded.

"I heard that Omar has plans to relocate to Harare," Hawa said.

"Business opportunity, surely," Rashid commented.

"Yes. Omar Bhai has a lot of hope for his grandson. He sees Hoosen as a disappointment," Hawa said.

"Why is that?" Rashid questioned.

"It's not fitting of me to discuss other people. I shouldn't have brought it up," Hawa replied.

Rashid nodded. He had come to know that Hawa trod very carefully. Her qualities were unique. She didn't speak badly of others and was always conscious of the impact of her words. He had learnt a lot from her qualities.

"Mama!" Salma called.

"Yes, my child," Hawa answered.

"When can I wear a *leebin*?" Salma, with her rosy cheeks and gentle curls asked.

"It's ribbon. RIB-Bon... not leebin," Saida, her elder sister scoffed.

"Don't be harsh, Saida. Your sister is still young," Hawa said, holding back a giggle.

"So, when can I wear one?" Salma asked, not fazed by her sister.

"Next Sunday. We are going to meet someone special. A little boy who is here from Aguutar," Hawa said.

"All the way from India? An India boy!" Hamza exclaimed.

"Hamza! Why do you speak that way? Your own mother is from India! Your father too," Rashid shouted.

"I'm not. I'm also not going anywhere to see some boy who probably cannot speak English. How old is he?" Hamza responded, cheekily.

"You will do as told! Your attitude, Hamza! I've been watching you and you speak back too often! Where has this arrogance come from?" Rashid asked, rising to his feet.

Hawa feared that Rashid may strike Hamza, so she sent him outside.

"That boy has lost his way already, " Rashid said.

"He is young. He will settle," Hawa affirmed. She had been concerned about Hamza's behaviour for some time. This was something she would need to work on.

"Now, count backwards from 100 in Gujarati. Not English!" a boy instructed.

Imtiyaaz began to count backwards in Gujarati. This was the third time in the last hour. Imtiyaaz was overcome with anxiety. It had been a few days since he'd reached South Africa and he was living with Bonny, his maternal grandfather. He had expected to move in immediately with his father, but that didn't seem to be the plan. He was surrounded by boys and girls – some close in age and some older – and they seemed fascinated by him. He was bilingual, but they insisted that he says things in Gujarati. They were generous with their laughter when he obliged.

Yasmeen, a tall woman with magnificent eyes and luscious brown hair, was kind towards him. She called him her grandson and she gave him special attention. He liked her and gravitated towards her, but his grandfather, in an attempt to force his integration, pushed him towards his aunts and uncles. Imtiyaaz wasn't sure if they liked him or if they just found him amusing.

They did things differently here. He asked for water, and it was received in a tumbler; poured from a pitcher. This was different to the clay pot in Aguutar. He had expected to bathe in a tub and had gasped for air and run out of the bathroom when water came through a nozzle. Yasmeen had picked up on the anxiety and had then taken him through the different things in the house and how they worked.

"Stop it!" a shy girl with short black hair shouted.

"It's enough! You are scaring him. Stop it," she said, taking Imtiyaaz by his hand.

Imtiyaaz looked at her gratefully.

"Come with me. I am decorating a cake. Come watch me. You can be the first to taste too," she said, with a warm smile.

Imtiyaaz looked around the kitchen. It was big, with tall wooden cupboards, a long table and little machines on the counter tops.

"They are called appliances," the girl said, catching his gaze.

"Appliances," Imtiyaaz repeated. "Ma showed me one that bread goes in. It comes out cut," Imtiyaaz continued, recalling his tour with Yasmeen.

"Yes, a bread slicer," the girl replied.

Imtiyaaz watched her put roses onto a cake. She said they were made from icing, and she invited him to taste one. It was sweet. Imtiyaaz had a sweet tooth.

"Tell me about my sister, Aaminah" the girl said.

"My Aaminah Khala is the best!" Imtiyaaz responded, overcome with sadness.

He missed his grandmother and Khala and he had been up last night, longing to be safe with them again.

"What does she look like?" the girl asked.

"Like an angel," Imtiyaaz confirmed.

She watched him tear up and she hugged him as he sobbed furiously.

A WARM GUSTY WIND FLOWED through the house. It was close to 33 degrees and Salma had fallen asleep clutching a piece of material. The material had been knotted at the top. She had created her own doll in this way. Hawa sipped on some water and then went to check on her son. He too was asleep.

Hamza had not been well for a few weeks. He had had scorching fevers, a general sense of malaise, and he had displayed shortness of breath in addition to having a runny nose. Hawa and Rashid had attributed the symptoms to the flu, since he had complained of a sore throat. Two weeks had passed, though, and he seemed to be worsening.

Hawa lifted his arm, which was hanging off the side of the bed and she caught sight of a fine rash. Hawa turned him over and she woke him.

"What is it, Ma?" he asked, groggily.

"My child, you have a rash. Let Mama see where else it is," Hawa said, anxiety rippling through her voice.

Hamza limply nodded and Hawa saw that the rash had appeared on his neck as well. Hamza coughed. Hawa hurriedly retrieved some calamine lotion and Panado syrup. She applied the calamine to his rash, but he had fallen into a sleep again, so she was unable to give him the syrup. Hawa settled onto the bed next to her son. She thought of the suffering that her children had to endure.

Her mind floated to Imtiyaaz and how afraid he had looked when he had met them. He had wide eyes like her friend Khadeejah, and he had spoken softly, just like her. Hawa had embraced him and introduced the children to him. His anxiety passed quickly, and he and the children had played for hours in the garden. He had been sorry to see them go. Hamza had played as well, and he had seemed to have forgotten his earlier misgivings. Hawa found herself deeply saddened. If suffering could be transferred to adults, she would gladly assume the suffering of her children and Imtiyaaz. She wanted only happiness and peace for them. Hawa's eyelids grew suddenly heavy, and she fell into a sleep.

Two men in white coats approached Hawa. The taller one had his eyes resting on the clipboard in front of him, whilst the other had his gaze lowered. They were flawless and their presence illuminated their surrounds.

"Tomorrow, you should take your son to the hospital. Fear not taking him, as his life is at risk," the taller man said, before leaving with the man who had accompanied him.

Hawa woke with a start. She looked around for the men frantically but soon realised that she was in her home. She looked to Hamza, and he looked significantly paler. Hawa instructed Saida to go to the shop and inform Rashid that Hamza needed medical attention.

It was minutes later that Saida and Rashid returned home and Rashid immediately saw Hamza's condition.

Hawa recounted her dream and Rashid rushed out of the house. Within twenty minutes he brought news that the vehicle would leave at 5AM the following morning for the hospital.

Rashid and Hawa had a sleepless night and it felt as if years had passed before 5AM arrived. Rashid carried his son to the car. Hamza did not stir. Despite the speed at which Rashid drove, the hospital appeared before them over two hours later. It was another hour before they were assisted. The nurses advised Hawa and Rashid that the doctor would see to Hamza and determine if any tests needed to be done. At this stage, Hamza's breathing was shallow.

Sunset settled without Rashid and Hawa moving from the orange chairs, and it was only then that a nurse appeared.

"Follow me," she said.

Rashid and Hawa quickly rose to their feet and followed her into the children's ward.

"Please put this mask on," she said, handing over two masks.

Rashid and Hawa obliged and Hawa's heart thudded in her chest. Hamza had been singled out in a room and the doctor watched his vital signs.

The doctor greeted Rashid and Hawa. They responded and he cut to the chase.

"We suspect quite a serious infection. It's a good thing that you brought your son in. We have started with basic treatment, but I will only have a clearer picture tomorrow," he said, firmly.

"Will he be okay?" Rashid asked, his voice shaking.

"I can't say that he will. Things aren't looking good," the doctor replied.

Hawa felt her insides turn. How is it that this situation had come upon them?

Rashid drummed his fingers on the dashboard and Hawa turned to look at him.

"The children are with my boss. They will be okay," Rashid assured her.

"They must be so worried, " Hawa said.

"Do you think that we should go back for the night?" Rashid asked.

"I am afraid to leave, in case..." Hawa stopped, unwilling to articulate her fears.

"We'll be back before he wakes up," Rashid finished.

Hawa mulled over his words, knowing that it may be that her son never wakes.

The couple remained silent throughout the drive, each captivated by their memories of Hamza.

"Where's Hamza?" Salma asked, fully awake, even though it was after midnight. She was seated on a royal blue armchair and her feet dangled above the floor.

Rashid's boss and his wife looked to Rashid for an answer, after explaining that Saida had slept after having a cup of milk, whilst Salma had insisted on staying up.

"Hamza has an infection. There's much to be done to try and help him," Rashid explained to his boss, careful not to say too much in Salma's presence.

"Will he be coming home tomorrow?" Salma asked, her little voice echoing through the room.

Rashid did not answer.

"Let's get you something to eat. Why don't you leave the children here tonight? It's important that you see to Hamza," Rashid's boss said sternly.

His wife, who had her hair up in a bun, nodded before inviting them into the kitchen. She had prepared roast chicken and roti for supper and had left their food aside, knowing that they wouldn't have eaten.

Out of politeness, Hawa and Rashid sat on the drawn-out chairs, but neither could stomach a meal.

Hawa and Rashid thanked the couple for their hospitality and kindness and asked Salma to stay over with Saida.

"I want to go home! I want to go to the hospital to bring Hamza home!" Salma whined.

"Salma! You will do as told!" Rashid admonished.

The exasperation slit through his voice. Salma began to cry and Hawa settled her before bidding the family goodnight.

Hawa and Rashid walked ten minutes through the dark to reach home. The house was unwelcoming and cold, despite it being summer. Hawa and Rashid waited for dawn, which eventually arrived, and the couple set out, both unsure of what news awaited them.

"Hamza had a difficult night. His breathing is very shallow," the nurse confirmed.

She was a tall woman with deep brown eyes.

"He is a little fighter though," a shorter nurse said with an encouraging smile.

"Doctor will be here shortly. You can see Hamza in the interim," the taller nurse said.

She was bending the rules, but she was sensitive to the couple's concerns, and she knew that they had travelled a long distance to be here. She was fully aware that Hamza may not live, and she didn't want to limit the time the couple spent with their beloved.

Hawa couldn't contain her emotion when she saw Hamza. His skin had a greyish tinge and his rash had spread to his face. He was attached to machinery and the nurse, seeing the panic in Hawa's eyes, let her know that the machine was causing him no pain.

"It's to assist with his breathing," she confirmed.

Rashid and Hawa stood around Hamza's bed, and it must have been an hour later when the doctor entered. He acknowledged them with a nod and asked that they step out while he examined Hamza. The couple obliged, but he left hurriedly following his examination without giving them an update.

Hawa looked to Rashid who seemed deeply angered.

"Damn doctor! He can't even talk to us like humans! It's our son!" Rashid exclaimed.

"Sir, doctor will be back," a third nurse informed, stepping up to them from behind.

Rashid opened his mouth to express his anger, but Hawa silenced him.

HAWA RAN HER FINGERS THROUGH Hamza's hair, waiting for the slightest indication from him that he knew she was there.

Rashid sat silently across the bed.

"The results have come in. I apologise about this morning. I had to rush," the doctor said, hours later, his voice breaking the silence.

Hawa's eyes met his and Rashid rose from his chair.

"Hamza has something called diphtheria. It's quite a serious infection. I will be able to ensure that he is treated accordingly, but it is my duty to inform you that there is a high possibility that he will not recover," the doctor said, bowing his head.

He didn't wait for a response before he headed to the nurse's island, giving them instructions. Hawa collapsed into her chair, her tears cascading.

"WHEN IS MY MAMA COMING home?" Salma asked, as she sucked a lollipop. She and Saida had been spoilt with sweet treats by Rashid's boss and his wife over the past week.

"When it is dark, just like yesterday!" Saida snapped.

"Why are you shouting at me?" Salma questioned.

"Stop asking stupid questions! You know Ma must be with Hamza. He is really sick!" Saida shouted.

"Settle down, children!" a voice called from the kitchen. The children immediately fell silent.

"Daddy has a rich boss," Salma said a few minutes later.

She had finished her lollipop and was now pretending to be smoking with the stick.

"Yes, he does," Saida agreed.

"Will Daddy become rich?" Salma asked.

"Maybe. Maybe one day we can have a house with a strong brown door. One with no cracks," Saida replied.

"Maybe I can have a real toy. A tea set!" Salma said, hopping on one foot.

"Stop doing that, Salma! And why are you pretending to smoke?" Saida asked.

"I see them smoking outside at night," Salma answered.

"Who is they?" Saida asked.

"Daddy's friends. The farm workers," Salma answered, confused that Saida didn't know who she was talking about.

"At night?" Saida asked, bewildered.

"Yes," Salma replied, "I will show you. Outside the window! Hamza goes there too!"

"Mama," a small voice called out.

Hawa leapt to her feet immediately and clasped her heart.

"Jee! Oh, Hamza!" Hawa cried.

"Mama, I want some water," Hamza said.

Hawa looked around and caught the attention of a nurse.

"My son! He wants some water. Please," Hawa called.

The nurse stared at Hamza in disbelief. The doctor had just said to them this morning that he was running out of options and that it would be a matter of days until he passed.

She brought water to Hamza.

"Here you go, brave boy," the nurse said, moving Hamza's hair to the side.

She helped him sit up and watched as he had a few sips.

A few minutes later, the nurse checked his vitals. His temperature was at the lowest since he had come in and the greyish tinge in his skin had been replaced with a pink glow.

"How are you feeling, Hamza?" Hawa asked.

Hamza looked around. He noted that the bed across him was empty.

"Am I sick, Mama?" Hamza asked.

"Yes, we brought you to hospital when your flu didn't get better," Hawa answered.

"Is Daddy here?" Hamza asked.

"He will come soon," Hawa replied.

Hamza nodded and he reached out to hold onto Hawa's finger.

"Don't leave me, Mama," Hamza said.

"It is you who shouldn't leave me," Hawa whispered as she stroked his forehead.

Rashid handed over a brass vase, one of his few family heirlooms to a fatigued man. The man pushed his spectacles further up his nose and without a word stepped back into an array of wooden shelves. He emerged a few minutes later with a wooden box. Rashid thanked him for his assistance and traced his fingers along a brass horse figurine. He recalled how he had demanded of his mother a real white horse and how she had indulged him, the first of many indulgences that had ultimately led to a dwindled estate. Hamza shared his love for horses, and he had asked Rashid for a toy horse months ago. Rashid, overcome by expenses, was unable to fulfil his request at the time but as his son lay in a hospital bed for weeks, he wanted to make good on his request. Gripped by expenses and a limited income, Rashid decided to exchange an ornament for a figurine. It was Hamza's first real item of value.

Rashid, despite assurances from the doctor that Hamza was on the road to recovery, couldn't dispense with the feeling that he had almost lost his son.

Rashid's boss, who had initially been understanding of the situation, had had his patience depleted. This was irrespective of Rashid returning to work four days after Hamza's admission, so Rashid had to secure transport to the hospital through a neighbour. The neighbour, a hard-working man who lived on the adjacent farm holding, had offered to care for the children and had wholeheartedly granted Rashid use of his vehicle. Rashid worked 10 hours at the shop per day, prior to setting out for the hospital in the evening. The anxiety and exhaustion were etched onto the faces of both Hawa and Rashid, but all that they longed for was the recovery of their son.

Hamza's smile grew when he saw the figurine in Rashid's hand.

"For you, my son," Rashid said, placing the figurine in Hamza's palm.

"A horse! Just like I asked for! Is it mine to keep?" Hamza asked.

"Yes, it is," Hawa responded, taking great pleasure in his happiness.

"Did it cost a lot of money?" Hamza asked.

"Not at all," Rashid replied, not regretful about the exchange.

"Mama. Dad. I want you to know that I want to work in the shop," Hamza announced, the conviction firm in his voice.

"Why do you want to do that?" Rashid asked, perplexed.

Hamza had spent some time thinking about his illness. The nurses had said that diphtheria can be caused from poor living conditions, and he feared that his siblings would acquire the same illness. There was also his smoking, but that would be stopped. Hamza felt that working would assist them with buying a home in a safer environment.

"I don't think school is for me," Hamza said.

"You will get well and go to school," Hawa said. "For now, just get some rest."

Hawa and Rashid headed home that evening, both waiting for the day that Hamza would return with them.

IMTIYAAZ DUG INTO HIS ICE cream sundae as he chatted animatedly to his uncles. Bonny closed his eyes for a moment and saw his daughter in the eyes of his grandson, heard her speak in the construction of his grandson's words, and felt her love in his innocent laughter. He felt pangs of guilt overtake him. He had had two beautiful daughters and a considerate and loving wife, but he had disregarded them under the guise of building a better future. He loved his new family immensely, but he felt that it was time that he showed a bit more attention to his family in Aguutar. He needed to put in firm steps to have them moved into Europe but, before doing so, he wanted them to visit South Africa.

"Papa! Are you alright?" his eldest son asked.

"Yes! Sorry! A day at the Rand Show sounds great!" he said, his eyes snapping open.

"We want to take Imtiyaaz to Carlton Centre too, and to the zoo! Let's make plans for every day of the long weekend!" his youngest daughter exclaimed.

"Of course," he said with a warm smile.

Bonny enjoyed many privileges and had acquired many pieces of land despite the white rule. He had the ability to network and was well-respected in the community. His wealth, however, did not serve as a rung on the ladder of arrogance. He remained humble and many approached him for assistance. He had assisted wholeheartedly and uplifted many struggling families through the provision of jobs, donations and loans. He just needed to extend this warmth to his family in Aguutar.

"Does Imtiyaaz have to move to Harare, Papa?" his son asked.

Imtiyaaz immediately fell silent. He had spent a few months with Bonny and even though the first few weeks had been excruciatingly difficult he had overcome them. The childish teasing had stopped, and each family member had welcomed him. Before long, they all competed for his attention, and he flourished. Imtiyaaz learnt new things each day, his etiquette developed, and he laughed freely. He still missed his beloved grandmother and aunt, and he would await their letters, which were read to him. Imtiyaaz asked to keep each letter and, even though he could not read, he memorised the words and ran his fingers across the writing, knowing that the ink had flowed from the pen held by his beloveds.

"Let's discuss that at a different time. Today is a happy day," Yasmeen said. Imtiyaaz had gripped her heart and she had already aired her concerns to Bonny about him moving to Harare. She didn't feel that it was in his best interests as Imtiyaaz's father's lack of interest in his son wasn't lost on her. She feared Imtiyaaz's fate and had pleaded with Bonny to stop the move.

He had shared in her concern, but he wasn't sure that his voice would hold against that of Omar's. They had claimed the boy as theirs and, even though Bonny was influential, he stood no chance against Omar.

HAWA PACKED HAMZA'S BAG CAREFULLY. He had been confined to his bed for a few weeks at home, but he had recovered. Hawa pondered over her dream and how she had almost lost her son. She saw him play with his horse on the floor and tears of gratitude honoured her face. Hamza would be back at school on Monday. He had fallen ill close to the end of the holidays and hadn't returned. He had four weeks of term left, but they had decided to let him go to catch-up. Hawa would miss him dearly, but she could cope with the temporary separation as opposed to the permanent separation that she had narrowly escaped.

YASMEEN DREW A WISP OF her hair into a ponytail before turning to look at Bonny, who was deeply engrossed in the morning paper.

"Today is the day," she sighed.

Bonny folded the newspaper in half and gazed at the concern in Yasmeen's perfectly featured face. She had taken Imtiyaaz on as her own grandchild immediately, and he had been rather astounded at the amount of care and love she gave him. It had been some time, but she had proven to him that she didn't harbour any malice in her heart towards his other family. This was a huge blessing and it made him love her more.

"I will do my best to convince him," Bonny promised.

Omar was visiting today to discuss Imtiyaaz's future. The hours dragged and Bonny wasn't surprised to see that Imtiyaaz's father was not present when Omar finally arrived.

"I'm sure Harare has got the better of Hoosen," Bonny commented dryly.

If Omar noted the tone, he showed no acknowledgement. Imtiyaaz had greeted his paternal grandfather with a hug and had run off to share the treats he'd received with his younger aunts and uncles. Imtiyaaz tried to push the thought from his mind that he would need to leave. He liked it here. He was safe and Bonny had promised to arrange for his grandma and aunt to visit.

He knew his aunt would like Joburg. She was an adventurous soul, and she would be keen to try all the rides that he had seen at the Rand Show. He wasn't tall enough to go on most of them, but he had had no issue in watching. He did, however, get to go on more height appropriate rides and had only grown nauseous once on the swirling teacups. How different this was to Aguutar!

"Bonny. Thank you for caring for Imtiyaaz. He looks like he has adjusted well," Omar commented.

Bonny cleared his throat and said, "He has settled well. The environment is good for him: children his age, Yasmeen's love. The structure. He is very happy here and he knows that there is a link to Aguutar here."

Omar had expected Bonny to take this line. "That's very well and good, but the whole idea of bringing the boy here was for him to be reunited with his father, grow up in the family home and one day run my businesses. He is the heir. My first grandson," Omar said, his voice thundering.

"No need to raise your voice. I am looking out for the best interests of my grandson," Bonny responded, angrily.

"And I am not? How dare you suggest that?" Omar questioned, his eyes glazing with fury.

"You know your son's failures. I've heard the stories," Bonny said, regaining his composure.

"I know my son better than anyone. The future of my family rests with that boy," Omar said.

"Business! Future! Reputation. What about his well-being?" Bonny asked.

"That's my responsibility. I came here to let you know that Hoosen's wedding date is set for three months from now. There's been a change. I have started working on Imtiyaaz's paperwork. He should be able to enter the country by the end of the month," Omar said, icily.

"What sort of change?" Bonny asked.

"I've been approached and saw a more favourable match. His initial engagement has been called off," Omar said.

"So, the rumours weren't rumours," Bonny muttered. "My daughter is dead. Your son didn't bring rainbows of joy into her life and in that way, she is better off gone. Halimah has filled me in. I now know. So, I couldn't care less which woman he marries but should any harm come to my grandson..." Bonny warned.

"Are you threatening me?" Omar said, jumping to his feet.

"I make promises, not threats," Bonny said.

Omar left without having lunch and as soon as the door closed Bonny began to weep. He wept for his daughter, he wept over his guilt, he wept for the boy who had been given to him as a second chance.

Imtiyaaz stared at his dhal and rice. Aasiyah, Omar's first wife, watched Imtiyaaz closely, but did not press him to eat. She had had no children herself and had encouraged Omar to re-marry for the purposes of having children. Omar had done so and had returned to South Africa: first with Hoosen, then with the remainder of his children. The girls were guarded in their interactions with her, but she was doing her best to win over their affection. Imtiyaaz remembered them from Aguutar, and he clung to them, but he had refused to eat more than a slice of bread each day since he had moved to Harare.

Imtiyaaz had not cried upon his separation from Bonny and the family as he had feared the look in his father's eyes. He had hidden his tears and his heart had been shrouded with anxiety throughout the journey to Harare. It was a long journey and for a portion of the journey the sky wept, giving Imtiyaaz the opportunity to see which drops of rain rolled down the window faster. Strangely enough, it was always the drop that started to roll last that reached the bottom first. Freedom doesn't always come to those who seek it immediately.

The girls had encouraged him to eat and had tended to him; choosing his clothes and showing him how his toys worked. Omar had showered Imtiyaaz with luxuries, from imported sweets to toys, but Imtiyaaz didn't seem moved. He wanted more than ever to return to Aguutar each time he saw the beady glance of his father. There were no exchanges of words between father and son, no smiles and no hugs.

Imtiyaaz sat on a red bench as his aunt did his laces.

"Can I ask you a question?" he started.

She looked up at him and he noticed the spread of freckles across her nose and cheeks. The heat had caused her skin to redden as well.

"I hate my freckles," she said, acknowledging his gaze.

"Oh, that. Oh, no. I want to ask you something, but you must promise that you won't tell anyone," Imtiyaaz said in a hushed tone.

"Sure," she answered and sat next to him.

"Fatima Foi, is my papa going to die too? Like my mother? Is that why he doesn't like me?" he asked.

Fatima, at a loss for words, stared into the wide eyes of the little boy. Her heart ached. "No! He isn't. He does love you. My brother is just a bit different. He loves you. That's why he brought you here to live with him. He goes to work in Big Papa's business for you," Fatima said.

"Oh," Imtiyaaz replied.

"Daddies show love differently to grannies and aunties," Fatima continued, wishing truth into her own words.

Fatima had noticed Hoosen's cold approach to Imtiyaaz. She wondered if he had married too soon. He had treated Khadeejah in a similar manner, but with her death they had all expected him to love his son openly. Fatima had tried to put it down to grief or uncertainty about being a single parent, but she had overheard her father insisting that the future was with Imtiyaaz and not "worthless" Hoosen. Fatima hadn't understood the comment and she feared asking, as it was not a matter of direct concern. She knew, however, that Hoosen rarely worked. He spent his time at bioscopes or with his friends: he had made a few of those very quickly in Harare. Fatima knew that life for both her and Imtiyaaz would be better in Aguutar, but destiny had brought them here, so here they would stand.

Imtiyaaz ate a plate full of food that evening, and both his grandparents smiled to themselves. Fatima was grateful that her words had had an impact. He had finally come around. Omar had arranged for him to attend a school two blocks away the following year and he knew that by then the boy would be settled. He needed him to settle. The family depended on it.

"Salma, do you think those people you saw outside were ghosts?" Saida asked, her eyes suddenly wide.

"When?" Salma responded, alarmed.

"The ones you saw outside with Hamza!" Saida said, now doubting the credibility of her sister's words.

"Oh! Those! No! I told you they are Daddy's friends. They work in the shop with him. You know. They carry boxes?" Salma answered.

"So does Daddy go outside with Hamza?" Saida asked.

"What are you two talking about?" Hawa asked, as she cut some spinach.

It was a huge blessing to live on this farm where they could grow their own food. The days of hunger had passed and Hawa was grateful each time she was able to prepare a meal for her family.

"Saida wants to know about why Hamza goes outside to see Daddy's friends at night-time," Salma announced, her curls bouncing around her face.

"Which friends? When?" Hawa asked, completely unaware of this.

"I saw him from the window once. You were all sleeping," Salma said, worried that she would be in trouble for peering through the curtains.

"Did you see it just once? Are you sure Daddy wasn't there? Was it not a dream? Tell me everything!" Hawa demanded.

"I saw him smoking with Daddy's friends. The ones from the shop! I saw it more than once," Salma said.

"Smoking! How do you know about smoking?" Hawa questioned.

"She does know! She pretends to smoke with her finger!" Saida jumped in.

"Salma! Smoking is a very bad thing! What nonsense is this?" Hawa said, angrily.

"I didn't do it for real, Mama. I just copied what Hamza did with my fingers and with a lollipop stick. Hamza's is real! He shares cigarettes and pipes with those people," Salma said, as she began to cry.

"Cry baby!" Saida jeered.

"Just stop!" Hawa shouted.

Her mind raced. She thought of Hamza lying in hospital. She thought of Rashid's sacrifices. She thought of her own. The doctor had said diphtheria can be picked up, it occurred in poor living conditions, unhygienic surrounds... Hawa, with the little they had, had always done her best to clean their home. She was pedantic about that. Could it be that his awful behaviour had led to his sickness?

Hawa massaged her temples. Hamza had gone off track. He was still so young and smoking. Smoke didn't cause diphtheria, but perhaps sharing cigarettes and pipes had. Rashid had a frightening temper. How would he react to Hamza's smoking? Would he beat him to a pulp on his return? Was her son destined for shame? Hawa swirled in these thoughts. Hamza was under 10 years old. If this was him now, Hawa feared what he may become later.

Rashid came home late that evening and Hawa was obliged to share her burden.

Rashid was silent and then spoke. "The boy has disgraced me. I work so hard. Poverty. Struggling. And now he is smoking," Rashid said. "I will break his bones! He will wish he died!" he yelled. "I'll get you all out of here! Rubbish! Weren't you meant to be raising them?" Rashid bellowed.

Hawa began to tremble.

"Sorry," Hawa mumbled before retreating into her safe place. She didn't hear the words and clutched to her tears.

IMTIYAAZ BOUNCED HIS BALL ON the pavement. He was grateful to be outside. The past week had been sweltering and his grandmother had insisted that he stay indoors. Omar showered him with luxuries, but it was his grandmother who took the extra care with him. She cooked things that he enjoyed, she spent time telling him magnificent stories, and she saw to his comfort. Hoosen had been travelling often to Johannesburg and Imtiyaaz had been quite comfortable in his absence.

His grandparents spoke of a wedding, and he had accompanied his aunts to the dressmaker who lived a block away. The wedding would now be after school started. A delay had arisen from paperwork, and Imtiyaaz wasn't sure what to expect from either set of circumstances. It would be nice to have a mommy, though. Imtiyaaz had befriended his neighbour, a little boy close in age, and Imtiyaaz had been enthralled with the way his mother looked at her son.

HALIMAH SIPPED ON HER TEA and watched Aaminah read the letter Bonny had sent. It was an invitation for Halimah and Aaminah's young family to visit South Africa for four months.

"Nothing ever changes!" Aaminah scoffed.

"Aaminah," Halimah reprimanded.

"Mother. Forgive me for my disrespect. My father, if he had read your last response, would have known that his grandson is just a month old and that I will not be able to travel for at least another 18 months. Yet, he insists on this visit. I think that you can honour this invitation, especially if you have an opportunity to see Imtiyaaz. I, however, cannot and he should know this," Aaminah said, carefully articulating her words.

It had been years since she had seen her father, but Aaminah had now accepted this. She had her own family now. She just hoped that her mother would not endure any hardship or pain from this visit.

Three months later, Halimah set off on her journey to Port Perowree. Aaminah and her husband accompanied her to bid her farewell. They all teared up and Aaminah felt her heart sink. She had never been separated from her mother and saw her every day, even following her marriage. There were planes which could have transported Halimah, but she had insisted on travelling by ship as she was nervous about Bonny incurring expenses. This had angered Aaminah further, but she'd held her tongue.

Halimah took with her gifts for his second wife, their children, and of course for her beloved Imtiyaaz. She had heard that he had settled into school well; he had always been a bright boy. She had heard also of the delay in Hoosen's marriage.

HALIMAH REMAINED SEATED AS THE vehicle came to a halt outside an impressive house. The house was adorned with French windows, and it boasted a manicured garden.

Saeed, Bonny's cousin, had driven Halimah from the port to Johannesburg. It had been a strenuous journey, and she was barely surprised that Bonny had made no effort to receive her himself.

Saeed got out of the car and Halimah was shocked when he opened the door for her. He opened the boot and left Halimah standing awkwardly outside the car. He led her towards the house and unlocked the door. They stepped into darkness.

"Bhai and the family will be coming tomorrow. They live in town mostly but would like to host you in the family home," Saeed said.

Halimah was dumbstruck. Was she expected to stay alone tonight, in a house in a foreign country?

"My wife has prepared supper for you at my house. If you prefer, we can leave your things here and I will bring you back in the morning," Saeed said, pity overtaking him.

This must be an overwhelming experience, and he could see how exhausted Halimah was. Saeed had been rather shocked when Bonny had asked that Halimah be taken to the family home, knowing that there would be no one there. Saeed's wife would have prepared supper and he was certain that his gregarious wife would not mind hosting a guest.

"Would that be an inconvenience?" Halimah asked, remembering her manners.

She instantly regretted coming to South Africa. This place was so far removed from her rural life in Aguutar, and her husband had opted to be cold, even though he had extended the invitation. Halimah felt like a burden.

"Not at all," Saeed said, plastering a reassuring smile on his rounded face.

Halimah watched as Saeed carried her luggage down the passageway. He returned and Halimah traced his path. She emerged a few minutes later in a plain navy punjabi, with a small bag. She had quickly packed an overnight bag.

Saeed's wife embraced Halimah. She enjoyed receiving guests and Halimah felt at ease within the first few moments. They gave her a comfortable room to sleep in and Halimah was pleasantly surprised to see a bathroom in the house. This was a far cry from Aguutar. The family home that she had been taken to was an even further cry. Her home in Aguutar could not in any way compare.

HALIMAH SMOOTHED THE CREASE OF her punjabi. Bonny had arrived with his eldest child. The greeting had been strained and Bonny had introduced her as Aunty Halimah. Halimah had smiled and been polite and they had shared niceties. The remainder of the family were arriving shortly, and Halimah assumed that Bonny had wanted to break the ice.

"What of Imtiyaaz?" Halimah asked.

"Omar has agreed to him coming. It's all arranged. If they stick to their word, he should be here tomorrow," Bonny said.

Halimah pursed her lips, holding her tears back. Oh, she would see her beloved! All this discomfort would dissipate on the sight of his silky hair and large, innocent eyes!

Car doors slammed and Bonny rose to his feet. He took charge of the situation; he would be facing head-on the consequence of his choices.

Yasmeen entered first; she looked sensational in a floral dress. Her eyes were accentuated by the subtle green hues of the dress and her hair fell in curls around her face. It took a moment for Halimah to realise that she was Bonny's wife. She was considerably younger than both Bonny and Halimah. Halimah, now conscious of her chapped hands, earned from hours of manual work in her farm style life, shook Yasmeen's hand. Halimah had aged, but she had once been a beautiful woman with auburn hair and light eyes but now she stood, almost ashamed, in the middle of the room.

Yasmeen gave Halimah a guarded smile and introduced the children to Halimah. The concept of "Aunty" was reiterated. Halimah felt as if she were in a different realm and was convinced that she would collapse.

The children eventually cleared the room, but Bonny's daughter remained. She could see a resemblance between Imtiyaaz and Halimah, and she wondered if it could be that this was the mother of her deceased sister. The mother of her living sister? It may be that they tried to protect the family by not disclosing the relation but this was the truth. It was not uncommon. There was nothing to be ashamed of. "Papa. Is this my mother?" she asked bravely.

Bonny looked at his daughter blankly. She always stepped outside of the line. He knew there was no point in concealing the truth from her; she was strong-minded.

"Sit down," he said.

Yasmeen felt discomfort and immediately tried to extinguish it. It was difficult to hear your child call your husband's wife "mother", but Yasmeen was a good woman. She would not allow the jealousy to control her.

"Aunty Halimah is my wife. We had two daughters, Khadeejah and Aaminah. Khadeejah has passed away. You probably know this… I did say Imtiyaaz is my grandchild and that you have a sister in Aguutar," Bonny said in one breath.

"Then why conceal Halimah mother from us? We all know we have a living sister. Today we met our mother!" she said, anger seeping through her voice.

"Our daughter speaks with wisdom," Yasmeen said, clasping her child's hand with that of Halimah's.

"Welcome to your home, Halimah," Yasmeen said, overcome by a range of emotions.

Imtiyaaz rubbed the sleep away from his eyes. It had been a long journey, and he was certain that he had seen steam rise from the road. The car had come to a grinding halt outside a house that he hadn't visited before. He had been dressed in a formal shirt and black pants; but the side parting that his aunt had created in his hair had disappeared during the journey. He had been told that he would be spending time with Bonny, but he wasn't sure why. He wasn't sure if Bonny had moved houses too, because he didn't remember this home in a picturesque suburb.

Halimah felt his presence before she saw him. She drank in his eyes, his tousled hair, and oh! How he had grown!

Imtiyaaz saw a vision of his beloved grandmother. Could it be? It was!

"Mama! Mama!" he screamed in delight as he raced towards her.

They clutched onto each other, neither able to comprehend the sweetness of the moment. Halimah pulled away eventually, but only to look at him. He had grown physically but she could see a maturity reflected in his eyes, a sadness.

"Mama, are you here to take me home?" Imtiyaaz asked, with an excited smile. Halimah fell silent. No one had explained to him that this was a visit. The men in this family had shielded themselves from difficult conversations, only to the detriment of the innocent.

"Come inside, my boy!" Bonny interrupted, even now affording only a distraction but no explanation. The pain of separation had ripped Halimah and Imtiyaaz apart; he was clearly unhappy but still there was no solution, no offer of hope.

Halimah had risen early to prepare Imtiyaaz's favourite meal, but she had felt hopeless. She wasn't sure about what most of the contraptions in the kitchen were. Yasmeen had come in to assist but neither were sure of what the boundaries were. It had been a strained few hours, and they had tried to make small talk, but the differences in their treatment by their husband and their lifestyle were clear as they moved around the kitchen.

Imtiyaaz clung to Halimah, day and night, and she had been forced to explain that she was on a visit. It would be a long visit, she assured him, but he had cried incessantly when he came to know that they would part again. It was in that moment that Halimah wondered if her coming to South Africa would cause him more pain.

"...it's polymorphic in nature," Ziyaad read, placing his glasses on the side table.

Ziyaad was the nerdy personality amongst Bonny's children.

"What's polymorphic?" his sister asked.

"It's like Imtiyaaz. When we first met him, he was quiet and wore *kurta* type things. An Aguutar boy. Now he is dressing like an Englishman!" Ziyaad commented.

"Why are you being rude?" his sister asked, angry.

"Why are they here?" Ziyaad asked.

"To be given an opportunity to be a family," Rabia responded.

"Is it really possible to merge the two?" Ziyaad queried.

"It should not be about merging what should already be seen as one entity," Rabia replied, vehemently.

Ziyaad nodded.

"I HAVE PINK RIB-BONS!" SALMA said, as she twirled around in a dress.

"We can see that. You look very pretty!" Hamza said, his heart bursting with pride. He loved to see his sisters looking beautiful.

"Come, kids. We have a long drive," Hawa said, her hair up in an elegant bun, supported by the only hair clip she owned. She wore a mint dress, having received the material as a gift from her aunt. The family settled into their neighbour's car, and they drove towards Lenasia. Hawa had been quite surprised that her family had received an invitation to Hoosen's wedding. Omar had known her family in Aguutar quite well, but she was taken aback that he had remembered her.

She had considered not attending, as it saddened her that Khadeejah had left this world and her husband was now re-marrying, but Hawa had chosen to attend for Imtiyaaz's sake. She often worried about his well-being, and she was seeking confirmation that his new mother would take care of him. Hawa, however, found it cruel that the wedding coincided with Halimah's trip to South Africa. It was accepted that her trip had turned out to be longer than expected, but Hawa couldn't imagine the pain she would feel recalling her own daughter's wedding to the same man.

Halimah felt her insides turn. She had not anticipated having to attend this wedding. She thought of how beautiful Khadeejah had looked when Halimah had pinned her bridal veil. She thought of the depth of her eyes, her wide smile and her gentle nature. Halimah bent over the toilet bowl and began to throw up.

Imtiyaaz looked impeccable in a grey suit. He wasn't sure of what the day would behold and found comfort in knowing his grandmother would be at his side. He folded up a picture he had drawn for his new mom. It had three stick figures and a heart. He had taken a great amount of time to draw it and he hoped that she would like it.

Zohra walked down the aisle. She was a beautiful woman, with luscious brown hair and light eyes. Her eyes narrowed as she saw a young boy seated at the main table. Was that her husband's son? Oh, the nerve! Did they expect her to sit near him? Why was he even at the wedding? Her smile disappeared as the crowd watched on.

Imtiyaaz dug into his pocket and smoothed out the picture he had drawn.

"That's a beautiful picture!" Halimah said, daggers piercing through her heart. She wanted nothing more than for Imtiyaaz to have the love of a mother, but she desperately wished that it was Khadeejah that the female figure on the paper represented.

"Will she like it?" Imtiyaaz asked, concerned.

"She will love it!" Halimah assured him.

She watched as Imtiyaaz bounded towards Zohra and his father. "I drew you a picture!" Imtiyaaz announced, now overcome with excitement. He thrust the paper towards Zohra.

She looked at him blankly and then at the picture. Zohra turned away from Imtiyaaz without a word. She would not be entertaining this rubbish, but she couldn't let him know verbally lest she be overheard.

"Do you not like it? I'm sorry! I can draw you another one. Sorry, I didn't mean for it to be ugly," Imtiyaaz whimpered.

"What are you babbling on about, boy?" his father reprimanded. "Go and play!"

Imtiyaaz felt his heart deaden in his chest and he hurriedly walked away to the safety of the outdoors.

"Don't worry about him; let's focus on us," Zohra's husband assured her, taking her hand. Zohra was fragile and he wished as much as she did that this was his first marriage.

"Why is it your father's wedding?" Salma asked, as her eyes settled on Imtiyaaz.

Imtiyaaz remembered the girl; they had come to visit him at Bonny's house. He didn't offer her an answer.

"I didn't go to my mommy and daddy's wedding!" she said.

"Salma! Why are you bothering Imtiyaaz?" Hamza admonished. "Imtiyaaz, do you want to play? We are going to play catch!" he invited warmly.

Imtiyaaz obliged and within moments he shrieked with delight. The innocence of a child.

Halimah watched him laugh from the wooden door.

She smiled. She loved to see him happy.

Imtiyaaz returned to Bonny's home with Halimah. He had had no further engagements with his father or Zohra. Omar had watched Zohra carefully throughout the function. She hadn't displayed any warmth towards Imtiyaaz. He had feared this, but he had already resolved that he would not allow Zohra to mistreat Imtiyaaz. The boy had a critical role to play, but he had already earned a dear space in Omar's heart. Omar would not wait to have this discussion; he would be addressing it upfront, as soon as the couple returned from their travels.

Halimah felt Imtiyaaz's grip tighten. He hadn't slept well the entire week and his behaviour had altered significantly with her departure being two days away. He had thrown tantrums and sat wailing in corners. Meals had been lost on him. Bonny, Halimah and Yasmeen had tried to ease his sadness, but these attempts had been met with violent tears.

Imtiyaaz had spent the bulk of the past few months travelling between Harare and Bonny's family home, and he had found a great sense of peace knowing that whatever difficulties were faced in Harare, his grandmother would ease. He had been enrolled into a school where he had faced mild bullying. Other children mocked his accent and he consistently had to explain why he had to walk to school and back, whilst other children were graciously dropped off and collected by their parents. Imtiyaaz was younger than his classmates, but his grandfather had been eager for him to start with his schooling journey. Omar had no intention of allowing Imtiyaaz to finish school, but he needed the basic skills to be learnt.

The day arrived too soon. It was a blistering day, and the skies were absent of chirping birds. The family stood outside, and Halimah shook uncontrollably as Imtiyaaz banged on the windows of the cream vehicle. His cheeks had reddened, and his eyes were swollen. It had taken three people to bundle him into the car. Imtiyaaz hadn't listened to any words of consolation, and he'd had to be physically pulled out of Halimah's arms. Bonny had insisted that she fly back to Aguutar, and they had felt it best that Imtiyaaz leave first. The car eventually turned onto the main road and Halimah was haunted only by his screams.

Yasmeen appreciated Halimah's gentle nature, and she was grateful for the time that had been spent. They had been able to share some moments of laughter but she was relieved that Halimah was leaving, and she saw the relief in the faces of most of her children as well. It had been an emotionally draining time. Nevertheless, Yasmeen concealed her relief and, when she bid Halimah goodbye, she conveyed that she was sad to see her go and that she was looking forward to future visits and the development of a solid relationship.

Halimah bade the family goodbye and Bonny drove Halimah to the airport alone. The silence was deafening but as he parked, he took her hand in his. "Make me *maaf*, Halimah. I promise to be a better husband. A better father. I will make the means to move you and our daughter out of Aguutar. I haven't been blinded to the difficulties you face," he said.

"My grandson. See to my precious," Halimah answered, his words coming too late. Love for Bonny was no longer something she concerned herself with. Her years had passed, and she saw how happy he was in the life he had built for himself. She had no place in it; nor did she seek a place. She closed her eyes ten minutes after the plane took off; leaving her grandson behind. Leaving South Africa behind.

AFTER LANDING, HALIMAH SETTLED INTO the vehicle taking her home, and her eyes rested on the dusty landscape. There would be an hour's drive home and she couldn't help comparing Aguutar to South Africa. Halimah wasn't attached to the world; she longed only for her grandson. Each time her eyes closed she saw their parting image. Her memory of his banging on the window coincided with the crashing of metal. Halimah's eyes snapped open and felt herself swirl into darkness. A shrill cry erupted from the vehicle, and Halimah felt herself slip into unconsciousness. Blood. More blood. Just like Khadeejah.

AAMINAH DRAPED HER SHEER PINK *odni* on her head. Her cheeks were sunken, her eyes bloodshot, and her clothes fell two sizes larger around her. It had been months since the devastating news of Halimah's accident, delivered matter-of-factly by an official in a khaki uniform, had reached Aaminah. Halimah, the backbone of their family unit, had spent weeks swirling in the mouth of death. Halimah, who'd once busied herself around her home, was now confined to a bed.

Aaminah's husband had graciously insisted on Halimah moving into their home after her lengthy stay at a state hospital. The medical facilities were amongst the poorest in the world and despite Bonny's efforts he had been unable to secure better medical assistance throughout the district.

He had arrived in Aguutar soon after the news of Halimah's accident had reached him. He had assisted Aaminah with caring for Halimah and he'd found himself engulfed in the depths of guilt as he watched his wife lie in her bed. Halimah hadn't lost her ability to speak, but her words were spoken in delirium. She spoke to Khadeejah often throughout the day, and if there were to be any virtue in the situation it would be that her daughter was alive to her.

Aaminah did not fear caring for her mother as Halimah would always be a priority to her, but it pained her greatly to see her mother in this state.

"Aaminah, take some rest," Bonny chided.

Aaminah wasn't sure how to respond to Bonny's presence. He had perhaps cared at too late a stage, as Halimah could not appreciate his presence. She had taken the role of a child, and it wasn't unusual for Aaminah to care for her children in the same way as she did for her mother.

"I am not tired," Aaminah said, firmly.

"You need to take care of yourself," Bonny replied.

"My wellness depends on that of my mother's. She is all that I have," Aaminah said.

Bonny felt her words slice through him. He deserved this, but it hurt.

"You have me. I know I haven't been present. I know I didn't provide for you fully. I mistreated your mother. I see my flaws and I ask you for *maaf*," he said, dropping his gaze to the marble floor.

"To forgive you is not within me," she answered.

"Perhaps someday," he said, the hope disappearing from his voice.

"You should go back to your family," Aaminah said, her eyes welling with tears.

"You are my family! I know it is late, but I am going to fight for this. I promised your mother that I would be there for her; here I am. I will not leave until her condition improves, until I can move you out of Aguutar," Bonny continued.

Aaminah wasn't given the opportunity to answer; Halimah had begun to screech.

HAWA STOOD, FOLDING HER DISH cloths at the kitchen table. Rashid had set out by train to fetch Hamza and Saida from their boarding house, a three-and-a-half-hour journey. It was Eid tomorrow and Rashid felt, as he had from the moment Hamza started schooling, that Eids should be spent together. Rashid had been forced to use the goods train. The fare was cheaper, and it was the only train available after eight. Rashid worked longer hours at the shop in recent times as Saida had begun schooling and, even though the *Jamaat* had provided the funds for most of the children's expenses, there were overhead expenses that Rashid needed to cover.

Hawa drew a sheet over Salma, who was sleeping soundly. She had earnestly awaited the arrival of her siblings and had refused to change out of her dungarees. Hawa had indulged her. Her daughter had missed her siblings dearly, even though she had befriended the daughter of a farm labourer. There had initially been a language barrier, but the girls had worked through that and had soon become good friends.

It was after midnight when Hawa heard footsteps. She rushed to the door and opened it prior to a knock. Hawa beamed as she gathered her son and daughter into her arms. It was an hour before the house fell into a treasured peace.

Hawa rose early to prepare an Eid breakfast. Rashid had managed to buy his children each a set of clothes: formal wear that they would need to use on this day and to any function held throughout the year. Salma and Saida were delighted with their lemon and white dresses and Hamza grinned when handed a blue shirt and black pants.

"Mama! I want *puri*! Why is the *puri* taking so long?" Saida whined.

"It will be done in a few minutes. Why don't you wash up?" Hawa asked.

"I already did! I'm hungry!" Saida squealed.

"I'm also hungry!" Salma chimed in.

"Shush. Just be grateful that we have food," Hamza said.

"Did I ever keep you hungry?" Rashid snapped.

Hawa held her breath.

"I was just saying..." Hamza explained.

"You were explaining nothing! Ungrateful fool! I work for you from dawn to dusk. You carry on like I kept you hungry!" Rashid yelled.

Hawa began to tremble. She had feared that there would be an outburst.

Rashid dragged the children into a room, and he was closely followed by Hawa.

"I will show you hungry!" he bellowed.

He locked his family into the room and the children's tears turned into whimpers. Rashid left the house and the food remained on the stove. The *puri* dough plastered itself to the kitchen table.

The day reached dusk and both Hawa and the children slipped into a deep sleep. Their Eid had been a day of fasting and there was no telling when the fast would break.

They had travelled only to be apart.

RASHID WATCHED THE BLOOD TRICKLE down his palms.

He had failed. Failed as a husband, father, and human being. He placed his life's events in scrutiny. He had had the opportunity to build a stable life, but he had lived a life driven by an attraction to satisfying his material desires and by doing so he had depleted his wealth. He had been forced to work exceptionally hard to provide a very basic standard of living for his family, and all other expenses had been seen to by charity. Rashid choked on a sob. His wife had been through so much in her own capacity. She hadn't really had a home and here he was, making her current home unsafe.

He had seen the fear in his children's eyes. His beautiful daughters. He had scarred them, and he wasn't sure what to do to redeem their trust. Would they expect this type of treatment from their own husbands someday? Would he allow his daughters to be subjugated to the same? Rashid felt his mind swirl in the disgust of his actions.. He vowed that from that moment he would not allow his own sorrows to be translated into abuse. His family would come first.

Rashid unlocked the door and fell to his knees. His children were sleeping and Hawa stared into the darkness.

"*Maaf*. Make me *maaf*," Rashid sobbed.

His body took over him and he retched on the floor. A damning pain sliced through his chest, and he gasped for air.

"Rashid!" Hawa screamed, scrambling to her feet.

"It's nothing. Stay back," he replied, breathing heavily.

He pushed himself off the floor and held onto the wall for support.

OMAR SHOOK HIS HEAD IN sheer disdain. "Is there any hope that she will recover?" he asked.

"It didn't sound like it. She is bedridden and her mental capacity has become somewhat challenged. She speaks to her daughter," Ismail Loonat reported.

He had arrived from Aguutar a few days ago and had taken it upon himself to share the update on his friend's former mother-in-law with Omar and Hoosen. The parties hadn't spoken in confidence and Imtiyaaz had grown pale. His lips quivered, but he was afraid to speak. Imtiyaaz feared both Omar and Hoosen, despite Omar showering him with gifts.

"To Aaminah? Well, I am glad that she can still communicate with her. The girl is fond of her mother," Omar commented.

"Not Aaminah. Khadeejah," Ismail said, pausing for dramatic effect.

Hoosen seemed unmoved. There was a sob from the corner of the room. "Boy! What are you doing listening in on adult conversations?" Hoosen growled.

Ismail smiled. He knew how much Hoosen disliked his son and as a man who had grown up with no family of his own, he took pleasure in this. Over and above this, Hoosen had basically been Ismail's walking ATM and Ismail had been nervous when the boy had moved to Harare. He believed that Hoosen would perhaps sway towards his son, but Ismail had been delighted to see that Hoosen had continued funding lunches at Casablanca Country Estate, gentleman club evenings and boy's fishing and hunting weekends. It was as if the boy didn't exist. Hoosen had recently started bringing his wife to the weekends away, though, which had annoyed Ismail and the wider friendship group, but as long as the money flowed, they didn't object.

"I didn't realise you were here!" Omar exclaimed.

Omar pitied the boy. Imtiyaaz loved Halimah and she was a link to the mother he had lost. It would be incredibly difficult for the boy to accept that Halimah could no longer care for him. He had essentially lost her fully, despite the distance and the fact that she lived on.

Omar placed Imtiyaaz on his knee, perhaps out of guilt. "I'm sorry you had to hear about your grandmother in this way. Just know that she loves you. Even now," Omar said, feebly.

Imtiyaaz could no longer contain his emotions and he wept. Hoosen and Ismail had long disappeared from the lounge and their laughter could be heard from the kitchen. A disgusting contrast.

HAWA DABBED AT A BEAD of sweat which had gathered on her brow. Temperatures had clocked in at close to 37 degrees. It had been months since Rashid had suffered a heart attack and it was only recently that his health had begun to improve. He hadn't worked, for obvious reasons, but his boss had paid his salary dutifully. Rashid had advised Hawa to save as much as possible lest he not survive. This had frightened Hawa, as she had no skills of her own and had not ever worked so she wasn't sure how she could support herself and three children should Rashid pass.

Salma had grown very attached to Rashid, for fear that he might leave her. She slept at his feet in the evening and played at his side during the day. Saida and Hamza were away at school, but the end of term was fast-approaching. Hawa would need to use the train herself, to travel to collect the children, but she was fearful of leaving Rashid.

"IT'S ALMOST THE END OF term. I'm sure your parents would like to see how well their little girls and boys can colour in!" Miss Hall announced.

She was a tall lady with aqua eyes, an ever-present smile, and strawberry blonde hair. She handed out sheets of paper with a picture of a bottle to the class, comprising about twenty students of different nationalities.

"There's a place for a message, so Mom and Dad can receive precious messages in a bottle from you," she said.

Imtiyaaz's heart sank. He stared at the piece of paper in front of him and five minutes later he hadn't lifted a pencil colour.

"Imtiyaaz, my darling, you have fifteen more minutes. Don't you like the picture?" Miss Hall asked.

Imtiyaaz reluctantly picked up a pencil colour, avoiding eye contact, and began to colour in the picture.

I love you, he wrote, as he had a wonderful idea. He would bury this paper in the garden; perhaps it would reach his mom in Aguutar. He examined the paper to ensure that he coloured within the lines. He had! She would be proud! He imagined her smile. He had created an image of her in his mind and she was always smiling, graceful and loving. A lot like Halimah. Imtiyaaz's heart sank again as he thought of his grandmother. He missed her and worried about her well-being. No news had reached him, though. It was as if she had disappeared from his life, albeit unwillingly.

Hawa packed Salma's clothes into a tiny brown suitcase. Her entire wardrobe comprised a lemon sun-dress, a pink formal dress, two pairs of dungarees, T-shirts, three jerseys and two pairs of jeans. Salma was starting school and it tore Hawa's heart apart to know that she would not see her precious little girl every day. She loved all her children, but Salma held a special place in Hawa's life.

Saida and Hamza now schooled in Belfast and Salma would be joining them. Rashid had regained his strength and was back at work but his boss, having indulged him with fully paid sick leave, had ensured that Rashid now put in the extra hours. He dutifully obliged, but he had been sorely disappointed that he had had very little time to say goodbye to Salma.

She had wailed as she'd boarded the goods train with her siblings and Hawa. Her siblings had tried to settle her, but the tantrums continued into the first month of term. The children stayed at a boarding house in a group of twelve other children. The children were accommodated in two rooms and had bathing facilities in an outbuilding. There was no heating of water permitted in the outbuilding and it was only once a fortnight that each child had the opportunity to bath inside with warm water. Hamza had taken on the extra responsibility of caring for Salma and he ensured that he cut her nails, filled her water bottle and braided her hair. Salma looked to Hamza as a parent, but he was no more than a child himself.

Hamza soon took on a job delivering vegetables and he saved the little money that he had. This was then spent on stickers for his sibling's books and school excursions.

OMAR RAN HIS FINGERS THROUGH his thinning hair. The business had done well this month. He'd received word that a block of apartments on Main Street was going on sale. That would be a great investment, particularly if he renovated the apartments and rented them out. This would have to wait until after his trip to London, though. He was taking a well-deserved holiday and was quite keen to allow Imtiyaaz some time to bond with his parents.

Omar had been firm about how he expected Zohra to treat Imtiyaaz and his fears had been eased as she had pasted a smile on her face and agreed to show Imtiyaaz love. Unknown to Omar, Zohra had a building disgust and hatred for Imtiyaaz, and nothing would have pleased her more than to see his demise. She had to conceal this from Hoosen's parents though, lest they force a divorce. She had much to benefit from this marriage financially, but she vowed to ensure that Imtiyaaz would have no role in her life.

Imtiyaaz wandered into the kitchen. It was 06h30. His grandmother usually prepared a hearty breakfast for him, but they had left for England the previous evening. Today, the kitchen was silent and not a slice of toast graced the table. Imtiyaaz wondered if his parents had overslept. He opened the fridge carefully and pulled out a carton of milk. He then walked over to the kitchen cupboard on the far right and located the Rice Krispies.

Snap. Crackle. Pop! The kitchen door banged behind him.

Hoosen, barely glancing at him, poured himself a glass of water. Imtiyaaz greeted his father with a warm smile. The smile wasn't returned. Zohra followed her husband into the kitchen. She seated herself at the table and Hoosen busied himself with eggs and a pan.

Minutes later, scrambled eggs and toast were plated, and the couple ate.

"Wash your bowl and cup," Hoosen instructed.

Imtiyaaz carried his dishes to the sink and began to rinse his dishes. Hoosen disappeared into the bathroom.

Imtiyaaz peered into the fridge and saw that his blue lunch box wasn't there.

"Looking for your lunch, you greedy little pig?" Zohra hissed.

Imtiyaaz felt his heart thud in his chest. He closed the fridge door.

"Go wake your dead mother up. She'll make it for you," she said, her words slicing through Imtiyaaz. She tossed her head back and laughed after she'd watched his face crumple.

Eight torturous weeks passed during which Imtiyaaz was dealt unimaginable blows. He hadn't had a proper meal and Jessica, the domestic worker who had pitied the frail young man, took it upon herself to share with him her already rationed pap and baked beans. There were no changes to their diet and the two of them would eat in silence after school, hidden amongst the trees.

Hoosen noted how frail the boy had become and, fearful of his father's reproach, he asked Zohra why this was so. Hoosen normally prepared breakfast for himself and Zohra, as he had noted that the boy preferred cereal in the morning. Had it been Rice Krispies that Hoosen had seen him eat innocently the morning after Omar had left?

Zohra had assured Hoosen that she served Imtiyaaz a hearty lunch and early supper and that he was probably losing weight because he was concerned about Halimah. Hoosen spent all his time with his friends, so he accepted the explanation. Zohra had also threatened Imtiyaaz, so Imtiyaaz did not dispute Zohra's version. Imtiyaaz did wonder, however, what he had done to earn her wrath.

A shriek escaped the bathroom and Hoosen, in a panic, raced to the bathroom door. "What is it?" he questioned, banging on the door.

Zohra opened the door and pointed to the ripped shower curtain and dead bird on the shower floor. "He did this! The monster! The evil child! I sit here and care for him and look at what I get? He is jealous of me!" Zohra yelled, placing her hand over her heart for extra effect.

Hoosen felt his blood boil. He took Zohra by her hand and led her into the living room. "I'm sorry. I'll deal with him," Hoosen said, patting her head.

Zohra smiled at her handiwork. It had been quite a challenge to smuggle the bird in without Hoosen noticing, but she had done it.

Imtiyaaz's tears spilled in disbelief as Hoosen hurled every insult he could think of at him. Hoosen ordered that the bathroom remain as it was: he wanted to demonstrate to his mother and father, who were arriving that afternoon, what Imtiyaaz truly was.

Imtiyaaz quivered as Omar's voice boomed. His grandparents had been led immediately to the bathroom following their arrival at home and, without questioning the veracity of the story they'd received, they had begun to cement the insults already hurled at Imtiyaaz. Zohra smiled inwardly. She finally had her pathetic in-laws on her side. Tonight would be the perfect time to share the news. She was expecting and she knew that the news would secure her a place in the family. She would never need to suffer the financial limitations she had back home. She planned on having many children, but she needed Imtiyaaz out of the way to make room for them. Her future would be through her children and for her children.

Imtiyaaz did not eat that evening and he had missed his lunch of baked beans that afternoon. He would be fed only through the salt of his tears.

Zohra lowered herself onto the brown couch after dinner and smiled at Hoosen.

Hoosen cleared his throat. "Ma. Papa. You are due to be grandparents. Zohra, however, has told me that she is experiencing some difficulties, so for the next few months, until after the baby is born, she is going to need to take it easy," Hoosen said.

Zohra had mentioned that she had gone to see a doctor following unusual bleeding and Hoosen had accepted the doctor's orders which, of course, Zohra had fabricated. She had been to the doctor for another reason, but that wasn't for Hoosen to know about.

Omar looked concerned and eyed Zohra closely. His wife shifted uncomfortably in her seat.

"What kind of difficulties?" Omar asked, not acknowledging the news of a grandchild.

Zohra felt annoyance graze her throat. "Bleeding!" she blurted. "But not to worry. I will do my duties. I can't expect Ma to do things. I just cannot deal with the stress that Imtiyaaz is putting on me. It's as if he wants me gone. He planned today so mischievously. I fear for my baby," Zohra said, pausing ever so often.

"What are you suggesting? That the boy is a threat?" Omar asked, incredulously.

"No. I. Just. I don't know! I do my best. I try. He is just jealous. If he could do this, he may try something else when he realises that I am here to stay. Me and my baby," Zohra said.

Omar rose from his seat. "Know your place. You and your child are at my mercy. I can throw you out on the street. Whatever Imtiyaaz did today, he has been punished for. He is a child! Don't create illusions!" Omar spat.

Zohra felt her plan begin to unravel. She forced tears but it was only Hoosen who comforted her.

THE RAIN POOLED AT IMTIYAAZ'S feet as he stood outside the back door. Zohra had given birth to a son and the entire family had gone to spend the week in Johannesburg. Omar, however, had arranged for the local Moulana to stay with Imtiyaaz for the duration of the week, as he had schooling commitments. Omar was pedantic about school attendance, the irony being in that he knew that he would pull the boy out of school at the age of 14. Imtiyaaz's aunts would be returning from Aguutar the following week and Imtiyaaz was relieved.

"Get in," the Moulana growled.

The Moulana, contrary to everything he was meant to stand for, was a bitter and greedy man. He had agreed to stay with Imtiyaaz only because he would be remunerated for it, but he had no intention of actually caring for him.

Imtiyaaz stepped in, his tiny feet leaving a trail of footprints on the kitchen floor.

"You are dirtying the house! You disgusting monster! Mother killer!" the Moulana yelled.

Imtiyaaz felt a hand come down on his back. Five minutes later, Imtiyaaz rocked back and forth, beaten by a man who was meant to care for him. Imtiyaaz shut his eyes.

"Mother killer. Mother killer. Mother killer," he repeated in sheer delirium.

Aaminah held onto Halimah's hand. Halimah had had a better few weeks and they had all settled into a new routine. They had relocated to central Europe. Bonny had been true to his word and had secured them a home. Aaminah had visited Khadeejah's grave site each day before they'd left Aguutar. She had been overwhelmed by their childhood memories, but she knew that, for her future and that of her children, Aguutar needed to become a distant memory.

Aaminah knew that she wouldn't see Bonny again but that was a fate that wasn't for her to challenge.

"Foi, did you see my Khala and Ma?" Imtiyaaz asked. The pair were seated on a green bench at a local park.

"I didn't. They have moved to a new country," came the soft reply.

"Where?" Imtiyaaz asked, feeling a sense of panic rise.

He had not been informed. Was Ma feeling better? Were they safe? Were they happy? How much had his cousins grown? Imtiyaaz longed for them every day.

"It's a place in Europe. I haven't ever been there," his aunt answered.

Imtiyaaz sat in silence.

"I miss them," he said.

"I know," she responded, draping her arm across him.

"Is Europe near or far?" Imtiyaaz suddenly asked.

His aunt, fearful of crushing his hope, stared at her feet.

"They live in your heart. Every time you want to be near them, you need to know that you are with them anyway," she said.

"Zohra hates me," Imtiyaaz confessed.

"I don't think so," his aunt answered.

"She does. I don't know why I am here. I want to be with my family. My Khala. My Ma," Imtiyaaz said, firmly. "Why can't I go?" he asked, his maturity evident in his voice.

"You are loved and needed here. We are also your family," she said.

"Maybe Zohra hates me because I am a mother killer," Imtiyaaz mused.

"What? Imtiyaaz! Where did you hear that? You aren't a mother killer!" his aunt responded, horrified. Her eyes had widened.

Imtiyaaz didn't respond to her.

"Imtiyaaz! Where did you hear that?" she asked again.

"The Moulana. He said I am a mother killer," Imtiyaaz answered.

Fury built within his aunt, and she immediately jumped to her feet. "I will be telling Papa!" she announced.

How much did this child need to endure?

Omar listened to his daughter's account. He walked out of the shop and crossed the road. He banged on the door of a cream house.

"Omar Bhai!" the Moulana said with a smile, opening the door.

"My grandson said that you called him a mother killer," Omar said, cutting to the chase. "Do you deny it?"

The Moulana felt fear rise within him. Omar was a powerful man. He hadn't expected that the boy would tell.

Deny. Denial would be the best way. The Moulana forced tears. "Omar Bhai! How could you believe such a thing? A man like myself? I treated him like my own son. He didn't want to pray. He troubled me. Even then I was kind. I would never!" the Moulana said. He looked for a recognition of sympathy in Omar's eyes.

"How could I have accused you?" Omar said, embracing him.

It was true. Zohra was right. Imtiyaaz was a dishonest, attention-seeking boy.

THE END OF THE YEAR had arrived, and the children returned to the farm with sunken eyes and protruding kneecaps. Rashid was aghast. He hadn't had much to offer them at home, but since their move to the farm they had been better nourished. He suspected that wasn't the case at the boarding house.

"Hamza, you are all so thin! Do you eat?" Rashid asked.

Hamza hesitated then answered. "They cook, but it's difficult to eat. It's things we don't eat," he answered.

"Like what?" Rashid asked.

"Like bony soup. A lot of it. Every day. Trotters. Then leftovers of the main house, served directly off their plates. Fried eggs for supper. " Hamza said.

"Every day?" Rashid questioned.

Hamza nodded. Rashid was overridden with guilt. He knew the *Jamaat* paid, but surely the children were entitled to basic meals.

Salma's eyes lit up as Hawa made cups of Nesquik. She hadn't had any kind of milk since her last visit home. She sipped on the milk and cuddled into Hawa. She had missed her mom terribly over the year and had even once started walking along the road, in the hope that she would reach home eventually.

There was a knock at the door. Rashid rose to answer it.

Pete, a burly man with blonde hair and emerald eyes, stood outside the door with his wife, Sarah. Sarah was petite, with auburn locks and well-defined eyebrows.

"Sir, is there a problem?" Rashid asked.

"I baked these," Sarah said, handing Rashid a basket of scones, muffins and preserves.

"Thank you," Rashid said. It was unusual for people of different races to have social visits, but Rashid stepped away from the door and invited them in.

Hawa smiled and asked them to have a seat.

"I saw you arrive with the children," Sarah said.

"We arrived in the morning," Hawa said. "They school a distance away from here."

Sarah had noted that the children looked worn out and had opted to bake for them. She had no children of her own and had often admired

Salma from her kitchen window as she ran across the farmland. Salma ventured quite far out onto Pete's private property, but they hadn't minded.

Pete and Sarah stayed for a while longer and Sarah offered to help the children get ready for bed. She was heartbroken to see their simple living conditions, a stark contrast to her own home.

Pete and Sarah despised the political regime, but as a farming couple they felt there was very little they could do to fight it.

"Join me at the auction tomorrow," Pete offered before leaving.

"I will," Rashid promised.

Rashid rose early and met Pete at the cattle auction. They stood side by side and it was only after it that Pete cleared his throat. "My wife and I don't have children of our own," he said.

"I'm sorry to hear that," Rashid responded.

"You have a special little girl. Would you ever consider allowing us to adopt her? We would let you see her. Shared custody. Anything, please," Pete blurted.

Rashid was dumbstruck. "My child is not up for adoption!" Rashid bellowed.

Tears sprang to Pete's eyes. "I'm sorry, I think... we are just so lonely. Desperate," Pete said.

Rashid was concerned about the desperation. He would have to instruct the children not to play in that area. "I understand. I am sorry for the way I reacted. I am sure you understand that my daughter is precious to me," Rashid said.

"I do," Pete answered.

"Sarah is welcome to visit with you some evenings," Rashid said, his heart softening slightly. He knew they wouldn't make off with his children in his presence.

"Thank you," Pete said in genuine appreciation. Limited time was at least some time.

PETE AND SARAH'S VISITS WERE frequent and the longing for Salma was evident in their eyes. This was not lost on anyone in the family.

"White people just want everything! Land. Education. Rights. Now even our child!" Rashid commented hotly, after they had left one evening.

"Why did you invite them into our lives?" Hawa asked.

"I pitied the man. I was afraid as well; that if I didn't, they would take Salma away," Rashid explained.

"I don't think they would. Their lives are here. They wouldn't sacrifice all that to commit a crime. Aside from that, this is apartheid South Africa. They would never succeed in keeping her. I think you worry too much," Hawa said.

"I have to protect my family!" Rashid emphasised.

"Then do so. I don't want to entertain these evenings. The children are leaving soon, anyway," Hawa said.

ZOHRA RUBBED HER EYES. "WHY did you book such an early flight?" she asked.

Hoosen was so careful with his beloved. He hoped he hadn't upset her. "I wanted us to reach Johannesburg fast so that I can take you shopping. A new wardrobe for your visit to the UK?" he suggested, with a grin.

"I packed my bags already! Why did you waste my time? I needed new things anyway! Unpack my bags!" she ordered.

Hoosen leapt to his feet.

Zohra grudgingly dragged her feet to the bathroom. She had to deal with his family, his lousy son, and now had to wake up early. They could have had a later flight. She didn't want to look tired when she arrived in the UK. She would make him pay – quite literally!

OMAR RE-LOOKED AT THE FIGURES. The business was in decline this month and there were large daily withdrawals. Hoosen! The lazy prodigal! He had withdrawn an enormous amount of money to fund his travel. To what length would this man go to please his young wife?

"You are doing so well! I can't wait to give Dad the positive feedback," Teacher gushed.

Imtiyaaz felt a familiar slicing through his heart. His father would not be attending his parent-teacher evening. He doubted if his father even knew who his teacher was. Hoosen had been on a six-month vacation, extended of course. Omar had become bitter as well. Imtiyaaz often heard screaming at home. It was something to do with money. Bonny would be sending a vehicle to fetch him, however, at the close of term, and Imtiyaaz was grateful for the escape.

Aaminah re-packed a shelf at their shop. Business had picked up over the past week; a great blessing, but she was tired out. She had her hands full with the children, the shop, household chores and seeing to her mom. She didn't see her mom as a chore, but her heart broke a bit more each day as her mom failed to recognise her. Halimah lived in the past. It was her safe place, and it was most disturbing that her illness had turned out to be the route to her own contentment.

Aaminah missed her mom's guidance, she ached for her love, and she felt now more than ever that she had lost all links to her family. Her letters to South Africa were unanswered. Omar had made a point of letting everyone in Aguutar know that Imtiyaaz was much better looked after now, and was healthier and happier. From an entire continent away, the traveller had brought the news and Aaminah had been told tales of how exceptional Zohra was. Aaminah knew that she and Halimah had done their best to care for Imtiyaaz and, even though she was glad that he was happier, she wished only for him to remember them.

THUNDERSTORMS DEVELOPED IN AASIYAH'S EYES. The violent rain began to fall as Omar's steely voice penetrated the room.

"I will give away this entire estate. You must leave this house! You aren't mine any longer! I cannot leave my millions to you. Yes, to my grandson, I can, but I know it will land up in your filthy and irresponsible hands so he too shall dwell without it," Omar said to Hoosen and Hoosen felt fresh anger towards his son emblazon his heart. How is it that he was more intelligent? He was just a child. What potential did he have?

"Please! Please! Don't disown my son! What will he do? He has no other home. No skill," Aasiyah pleaded.

"Aasiyah! This matter does not concern you!" Omar screamed.

"My son. My son!" Aasiyah screeched.

"Your son? You benefited from his birth by another woman. My other wife. He is not your son as much as he isn't entitled to my estate! A prodigal! A waste of air! An embarrassment!" Omar bellowed, delivering a blow with his words.

Aasiyah's face crumpled but Omar did not flinch. His entire business reputation was at stake because Hoosen had been spending incessantly without caring for the business. To make matters worse, they had lost a government tender for the provision of mining uniforms because of Hoosen's recklessness. The line had to be drawn. Omar slammed the front door behind him, and the house settled into an uncomfortable silence.

MONDAY DAWNED BUT IMTIYAAZ COULD not find his school uniform.

He wandered into the kitchen and tugged at Aasiyah's maroon printed dress.

"Dadi. Assalaamu alaikum," he said, gently.

His grandmother had enveloped herself in silence since the weekend's debacle.

"My child, *wa alaykum salaam,*" she whispered.

This wasn't her grandson, though. Omar had made it clear that she had no rights over the children or grandchildren of this household. Steady tears filled her eyes and Imtiyaaz immediately hugged her. He understood. He too had heard the exchange of words.

"I can't find my uniform," he said, finally withdrawing from the embrace

Aasiyah's breath caught in her throat. How would she tell him?

"Papa, he decided..." Aasiyah began.

Imtiyaaz searched her eyes.

"You are needed at the shop," she finished.

"NO! I will not! No!" Imtiyaaz yelled, and he bolted out of the door.

He found himself at school with no uniform. It was week four into term one and Imtiyaaz had left Bonny's house after the holidays, looking forward only to school. This was his purpose.

"Imtiyaaz, where is your uniform?" Teacher asked.

"I don't know, Teacher. My grandfather took it. He doesn't want me to go to school. He wants me to run his shop!" Imtiyaaz wailed.

"Of all the excuses," Teacher responded.

She then gazed at him and noted the panic in his eyes.

"Come. Let's go to Mr Harrison's office," she said, taking his hand.

Mr Harrison was a tall, impeccably dressed man. He looked to be regal but, as Imtiyaaz entered his office, his face softened. He had heard about the loss the boy had suffered, he knew about his great intellectual capacity, and he had been told of Imtiyaaz's gentle character. The boy was dressed in plain clothes, and he hoped that Teacher Halford hadn't brought the boy in to be disciplined. He sighed inwardly.

"Sir, we have a bit of a problem," Teacher Halford began.

She hadn't experienced a similar problem before, but she recounted the facts and Mr Harrison felt his heart sink.

The three souls patiently awaited the arrival of Omar. Mr Harrison had telephoned him, but an entire hour had passed. Teacher Halford had given the reigns to the assistant teacher. She felt that she needed to support Imtiyaaz through this, and she entertained him by telling him tales of her pet rabbit.

Omar entered the office just before 11, and his presence shook Imtiyaaz.

"Ah, you have gathered my grandson for me. Apologies: I didn't have the time to inform the school that Imtiyaaz will no longer be attending classes," Omar said, coolly.

"Will Imtiyaaz be attending elsewhere? We can assist with a transfer, even though it would be a sad day to lose our star pupil," Mr Harrison asked, fully aware that there would be no transfer.

"That won't be necessary. Imtiyaaz doesn't need to pursue any further formal education. I know fees have been paid up for the year. Consider the rest a contribution to the school," Omar said, his voice hard.

"You can't just do that! This boy has so much talent. He could someday be an accountant, doctor, or lawyer," Teacher Halford exclaimed.

"Oh, can't I? The boy is mine. I can do with him what I please. He is going to be a businessman. Run my empire!" Omar shouted.

"Run your empire? He is a child! He doesn't have the capacity to run your empire at this point!" Mr Harrison responded.

"Were you not just singing his praises? Suddenly he doesn't have capacity!" Omar scoffed.

Mr Harrison stood squarely. "It is in the best interests of Imtiyaaz to continue schooling. I will approach the authorities should you stand in the way," Mr Harrison threatened.

"On what basis? There is no law compelling him to further his schooling. This is a private institution! Above all else," Omar said, not backing down.

Mr Harrison knew he lost the battle. "Very well," Mr Harrison said.

Teacher Halford began to sob and Imtiyaaz appeared as pale as an ice sculpture. School. He loved school. This was all he had.

Omar cleared his throat and Imtiyaaz slowly rose. The pair left the office in silence.

"I have an idea," Teacher Halford began. "I could find him and offer him free classes in the afternoon. Hidden classes."

Mr Harrison did not answer. He was in deep thought. He thought of his own father, an uneducated fisherman. His father had often stressed their education, living by the mantra, "it takes an uneducated man to know the value of education."

IMTIYAAZ DRUMMED HIS FINGERS ON the counter top. It had been a long day, a long week, a long month, and a long five years since he had joined the business. He had thrown tantrum after tantrum when pulled out of school; he had had hidden classes; he had even bought a train ticket to flee his miserable life, but eventually he had stopped trying. He accepted his fate and dreaded only the evenings when he had to return home. He had multiple half brothers and sisters now, but his stepmother ensured that both they and he knew that there would be no relationship.

Bonny had made an unsuccessful bid to adopt him a few years ago and whereas, whilst he was schooling, he had been able to spend school holidays and the occasional long weekend with Bonny and his beloved family, he was now bound to the business and in recent years had seen them for a week at a time, biannually.

Age seemed to have taken over and Omar's vibrancy had dimmed, particularly over the last month. He had struggled with heart disease and Imtiyaaz had tried to make light of the situation by attributing it to all the *gulab jamuns* and ghee rotis that his grandfather had consumed, but in truth Imtiyaaz knew that Omar was under pressure. Hoosen had proven to his father that he had no financial acumen and he followed only the whims and demands of his unruly wife. Omar had eventually caught on to her nature but, for the sake of his grandchildren, he had learnt to control his tongue. Omar found peace only in knowing that Imtiyaaz was capable, and it was only occasionally that he experienced tornadoes of guilt for pulling the boy out of school. It had been his only option, though.

"Imtiyaaz! Imtiyaaz! Come quickly!" a shrill voice belonging to their domestic worker rang out. She had a pained look in her eyes, and he was certain that she had run a few blocks to reach him.

"What is it?" Imtiyaaz asked, his eyes widening.

"Papa! He fell!" Jessica screamed.

Imtiyaaz felt his heart hammer in his chest and his tummy churn. He followed Jessica at full speed, but he knew what he would find when he reached home.

Dr Masea got off his knees before pushing Omar's eyes closed. "He's gone," the doctor said, sadness creeping into his voice. Omar had been his friend; he had even lent him money to purchase medical equipment for his medical practice on the upper end of town.

The household erupted into tears with the exception of one: the new lady of the manor. She smiled outwardly. Her life was about to get better.

"WHY ARE YOU TORMENTING YOURSELF, Hawa?" Fazila, a softly featured lady asked.

"I don't know what to do about Hamza. My fear is that he doesn't come back on track," Hawa said.

"Don't exaggerate. All he did was slip out of the boarding house," Fazila said.

"To smoke and get involved with the wrong crowd," Hawa said, sighing deeply.

"He is young. It isn't the end of the world," Fazila assured Hawa.

"Rashid wants to drag him into shop work. Take him out of school," Hawa said.

"That hardly ever works out. Look at Khadeejah's boy, Imtiyaaz. They ruined his life by forcing the business on him," Fazila said.

"My heart bleeds for him each day. Khadeejah would not have wanted this," Hawa said, sadly.

"I just wish there was some sort of contingency plan for him. Something for him to fall back on later in life, should something happen," Fazila said.

"What more could happen to that precious boy? I am sure that all that is ahead for him will be beautiful," Hawa said.

IMTIYAAZ WALKED OUT OF THE masjid and shielded his eyes from the sun. It was a scorching day, and he had taken refuge in the safety of the masjid, the only place where he found peace. He began to walk towards the shop, grateful for the occasional shade given by scattered trees. He thought of how Zohra had hit his grandmother the previous week, and then he reflected on how his father had remained silent. Imtiyaaz had been the courageous one and had stood up to her. His father had been icy toward him since, but Imtiyaaz could not fathom how Zohra's disrespect to an aged woman, a gentle woman, could be tolerated.

He turned the corner and stepped onto the pavement. It was then that he felt a firing of stones against his back. It was rhythmic at first and then haphazard as stones and larger rocks were flung incessantly at him. Imtiyaaz scrambled into a nearby bush for cover. His heart rate rose, and he examined the steady rivers of blood flowing down his body. His shirt had been ripped but he hadn't had a moment to recover before the perpetrator stood laughing in front of him. Her hair was flying wildly around her, and her eyes shone with hatred.

"My life's purpose is to destroy you," Zohra gleefully announced.

Imtiyaaz stared at her, a paragon of evil, before attempting to defend himself. "What's the matter, boy?" she taunted, "Can't stand up to a lady? Did you forget how you rushed to aid the old hag last week?" she said, in a sing-song voice.

Imtiyaaz's vision blurred as he felt a blow levelled at him. He was floating, through anger, through physical pain, and then finally into darkness.

The doctor glanced at Imtiyaaz. "Your wounds will heal," he advised.

The doctor had chosen to not listen to Imtiyaaz's explanation of how he had been stoned. He was, after all, a friend of the family and Hoosen had not yet claimed the outstanding monies owed by him for the new medical equipment. Hoosen was far easier to use than a bank. Omar had helped him, but he had been tougher on repayments. The talk of the town was that Hoosen had lent out over a million to a friend to start up a supermarket. The payment terms were loose. No, no, no. He had to not only turn a blind eye to the cause of Imtiyaaz's wounds but, should he be asked about it, he would fabricate a report. There was no need to alienate Hoosen by causing problems in his marriage.

"How can you allow him to accuse me? "Zohra wailed. She paced around the room and skilfully managed her tears.

"I believe my grandson," came a quiet yet determined voice." He is the only one in this home who saw right through you from the very beginning. I wish Omar had taken action!"

Hoosen's fury was now unleashed. How is it that an innocent woman, his beloved wife, could be accused of this? "The medical reports are clear! You heard the doctor. This boy was trouble from the moment he was born! He will not be destroying my life! From now on, no mercy. His treatment will be determined by my wife, and I will hear nothing further," Hoosen spat scathingly.

Imtiyaaz's patience had worn out. He didn't need this. He had been used and abused and the line had to be drawn. He was done. Done. His father had chosen his path and now he had to choose his and it did not include this.

He walked purposefully out of the lounge and into his room. It comprised a single bed and a wooden wardrobe. His furniture, his ornaments and other items had disappeared gradually and now graced the rooms of his so-called siblings. They had fired angry gazes at him and the eldest had pulled a face, cursing him. It was Imtiyaaz who earned their bread and yet he was exposed to emotional and physical abuse. He had been blamed for his mother's death time and time again, and now he openly wondered why he too had not passed on that dreadful day.

Imtiyaaz moved systematically and it was only once he got onto the bus that he realised that he had seen hatred in his father's eyes.

Yasmeen flew into a panic when she saw the state of Imtiyaaz as he stood at the door. His eyes were puffy, his lips were drawn, and his wounds were prominent.

"My boy! What happened? Quick! Come in," Yasmeen screeched. She fussed over him, and the lounge filled with his aunts and uncles.

"That woman! Enough is enough!" Yasmeen screamed.

Yasmeen considered Imtiyaaz to be her eldest grandchild. He had won her heart and she loved him dearly. It had crushed her when the bid to adopt him had failed. She was constantly worrying about him and now she saw that she had a reason to.

"What's going on here?" Bonny asked as he entered the room. His eyes scanned the worried looks and finally rested on his grandson, lying helplessly on the paisley couch.

"Imtiyaaz! Are you okay?" Bonny questioned, rushing to his side.

"Better than I was," Imtiyaaz said, forcing a smile. He pushed himself up, but the physical pain and emotional trauma had finally fully set in.

"What is the meaning of this? What happened? Who is responsible? How did you get here?" Bonny asked, without pausing for a breath.

Imtiyaaz and Yasmeen carefully and truthfully answered his questions and Bonny felt his heart rip into shreds. How had he allowed this to go so far?

"You will not go back. I will get the evidence we need," Bonny resolved.

"Papa, they have me trapped. The doctor himself is their pawn. Who will believe me?" Imtiyaaz asked. The desperation was apparent in his voice.

"We believe you," Yasmeen said.

There was a chorus of agreement in the room.

"Papa, I know we discussed it before. I know my grandfather would not allow it. He is gone now. I would like to see Mama and Khala," Imtiyaaz said, a firmness in his voice.

Yasmeen and Bonny glanced at each other.

"We will discuss it," Bonny said. "For now, let me have you seen to. Maybe a new doctor's report will prove things," Bonny said.

Bonny and Yasmeen stepped into the entrance hall and Bonny called his family doctor.

"You should honour his wish," Yasmeen said.

"Halimah will not recognise him. Aaminah has distanced herself from me," Bonny mentioned.

"Is this about your relationship with your family? Or is about Imtiyaaz?" Yasmeen asked. She was no longer afraid to question him.

"You know what Omar said. The threat! You know how awful Imtiyaaz would feel to see that his aunt has moved on; that his mama doesn't recognise him?" Bonny said, growing defensive.

"He has seen a lot more. This will be good for him. Omar is deceased. There is nothing to fear. Even when he was alive, you caved in for no reason!" Yasmeen blurted.

Bonny remained silent and walked back into the lounge.

"The doctor will see you this afternoon. Then we can talk about your trip," Bonny said.

Imtiyaaz's face lit up. He would be reunited at last.

Bonny pressed an envelope into Imtiyaaz's hand.

"For your aunt," Bonny said, somewhat gruffly.

Yasmeen did not know what the contents of the envelope were, and she brushed her curiosity aside. Her husband had a family, and she did not need to know every detail of his relationship with them. She had spent earlier years convinced that she was dearer to Bonny, more deeply loved, and more greatly cherished and, although this was all true, she realised that Halimah occupied a different part of his heart. She had seen his guilt and pain the last time he had parted from Halimah.

Yasmeen was removed from her thoughts only when Imtiyaaz embraced her. "Be safe, my dear boy," she whispered before she planted a kiss on his forehead.

The couple waved at him as he headed towards the check-in counter.

AAMINAH HAD BEEN UP TENDING to Zakiyya's fever the night before. She needed to be at the airport by 11 to collect her nephew and there was still a school run to get through. She was exhausted and, admittedly, overwhelmed. It had been years since she had last seen Imtiyaaz, but she prayed for him daily, even though there was no contact between them. She had been rather surprised that he had opted to travel to see them, especially after she had been informed numerous times about how blissfully happy he was. She had heard about Omar's death, but this was accompanied by the news that Imtiyaaz had opted to take on the family business and that he spent his weekends on fishing trips with his siblings and father whilst Zohra took care of the business. Aaminah had also heard about how much he loved Zohra and how he had no desire to maintain links with his past.

In any case, Aaminah could not close her door on him. She would welcome him, despite his viewpoint. Aaminah then thought of Bonny and wondered if this was a ploy for Bonny to re-enter her life. Perhaps Bonny thought that reuniting aunt and nephew would open the doors of forgiveness. He was wrong. She had already forgiven him, but she had no place for him going forward. The abandoned would now abandon.

Imtiyaaz's large eyes searched the baggage carousel and his eyes finally landed on his navy hardtop Delsey suitcase. He hurriedly lifted it and put it onto his fairly empty trolley. His heart was now racing. Would he recognise Khala? Would she recognise him? Why had she stopped writing letters?

These questions whirled through his mind as he stepped out of the automatic doors. There was a sea of faces around him, and he stepped around a tour group. Imtiyaaz felt his heart sink to his knees. She had not come. The sadness turned into panic. He was in a foreign country on another continent, and he didn't know where to go. He leaned against a pillar for support.

Aaminah turned the corner and her eyes searched frantically for her nephew. She was close to an hour late, but traffic had been nothing short of nightmarish and her taxi driver hadn't seemed at all interested in finding a quicker route. She saw grandmothers clinging to their grandchildren, laughing couples, and then she saw a boy slumped against a pillar. His head was down but she couldn't have mistaken that shiny hair for anyone else in the world. Tears sprang to her eyes as she approached him.

"Imtiyaaz?" she called out.

The boy lifted his head, and she was taken back in time to when those magnificent eyes had looked into hers questioningly when she hid his favourite toys to tease him.

"Khala," he said.

He had waited and gone through so many emotions that his excitement had worn off.

"Yes," she said.

They stood awkwardly and then he latched onto her. She felt her disappointment in him fall away. How could a boy as innocent as him say such hurtful things and cut contact? She allowed her thoughts to roam freely but then she fiercely reminded herself that she must not give too much of herself. The reason for his visit was unclear and she did not feel like harming her weakened heart.

"How is Mama?" he asked as he let go.

Aaminah hesitated. "She is coping. Things are different to when you last saw her. The accident did take a toll," she replied.

Imtiyaaz remained silent. He had hoped that things wouldn't be too bad. He had imagined walking in to see her smiling face. This fantasy had given him hope. Hope kept him alive.

The drive to Aaminah's house was picturesque. The traffic had subsided, and he took in the rolling hills, the grazing sheep and the crisp blue sky as soon as they turned off the highway.

Aaminah pointed out landmarks, but Imtiyaaz barely heard her as he was concerned about how different things felt. The car pulled over outside a brick double-storey house sometime later. There were three stairs that led to a wooden front door. The cab driver politely carried Imtiyaaz's bags up the stairs. Aaminah tipped him generously and pushed the front door open. Six pairs of eyes earnestly stared at Imtiyaaz, and he recognised a set immediately. He fist pumped each of them before turning to Aaminah.

Knowingly, she led him to a room on the far left. There was a woman sitting upright against a padded headboard. She looked straight ahead and didn't turn at the sound of voices. Imtiyaaz saw his beautiful Mama. He drank in her vision. He didn't see her wrinkled hands or tired eyes. He saw the woman who'd loved and raised him.

"Mama!" he said.

She turned towards the door.

"Khadeejah. Your boy is here," Halimah said.

Aaminah did a double take. Her mother had recognised him! She knew. But how?

Imtiyaaz and Aaminah rushed to her side.

"Mama! You are here with us!" Aaminah squealed with delight.

Halimah stared blankly. "Imtiyaaz. He is here. Imtiyaaz," Halimah said, repeating her sentence multiple times.

"I am here," Imtiyaaz assured her, his voice overcome with emotion.

He cried freely as he clung to her, but she shared no other words. It was enough that she remembered. It was enough that she knew he'd come back.

Imtiyaaz rose with the sun and saw that he was in a foetal position at the foot of Halimah's bed. He had stayed awake for most of the night, trying to talk to her, but his conversations were one-sided. Aaminah had left them to tend to her children, her husband, and her chores, but she felt burning questions rise within her. Why now? Why after all these years? Why after all the disappointment? She would ask him, she resolved. First thing in the morning or at least after her school-going children were at school.

Imtiyaaz patted Halimah's hand but she continued to sleep, breathing deeply. He found himself across from Aaminah in the kitchen a mere two hours later. He had retrieved the envelope from Bonny, and he carefully handed it to her. Aaminah immediately recognised her father's hand, and she felt rage rise in her.

"Is he why you are here?" she asked, flames dancing through her eyes.

"What? No! Well, he arranged for my trip but only after I begged him to come," Imtiyaaz responded, alarmed by her anger.

"Then what is this? And why would you beg him to come? You were all fine and good. I heard what you said. That you have a life with *your* family, which is better than what my mother and I could give you!" she yelled as she flung the envelope across the kitchen.

Imtiyaaz's head began to spin. He hadn't imagined her attitude; something had been amiss. "Khala, what are you saying? Where did you hear this?" Imtiyaaz asked, clinging to the side of the wooden table.

"So, your grandfather died and now you are the big man who can take his place? So, you come here and give us hope that you are back? You give Ma a reason to live, and we don't know why? You abandoned us!" Aaminah shouted, her tears drying instantly on her warm cheeks.

Tears and tears. Where was the butterfly to catch when all they did was gather their own tears and the tears of others?

"Khala. I didn't come here to upset you. I don't know what you have heard. I am a slave. I was a slave to my grandfather. He forced me out of school to look after his business. My father takes on no responsibility. He hates me. I have known no love from him. My stepmother? Ha! She hates me. Abuse? Not just emotional," Imtiyaaz said. He rolled up his left sleeve to show Aaminah his scars.

"These? These are from when she stoned me. No one believed me, so I fled to my grandfather. Bonny! I begged him to let me come to you. To Mama. It wasn't easy for him. But here I am," Imtiyaaz said, bravely.

Aaminah was dumbstruck. She stared at the damaged skin of the boy whom she had tried so hard to protect. She had failed.

Imtiyaaz began to fill Aaminah in on his years. He spoke to her of how he'd awaited her letters and how they hadn't arrived. He expressed his deepest sorrows about his ill-treatment and about how his father was unstoppable in his quest to please his beloved wife.

Aaminah felt her anger give way to guilt. She had questioned her blood. She had believed the words of others ahead of searching for the truth. She had allowed her sister's son to be abused. She began to tremble and Imtiyaaz held her. "You're here now, with us," she consoled him, not realising that he was in fact consoling her.

"I am here," he repeated, as he had the previous night.

Zohra admired her handiwork time and time again. Her husband was closer to her than ever, and she was more than ready to suggest to him that he make a move to find out what exactly his powers were for amending his father's Trust. She had succeeded in drawing him the furthest away from his son as possible, and she had convinced him that the local *Qari* was more than capable of running the business. Who cares that the "mongrel" had run away? she had asked him the previous night. He was only good gone.

She would make sure that she and her children became the sole beneficiaries of the empire and there was nothing better than Imtiyaaz's absence to achieve this. She would be a millionaire. She would tour the world, dine and never have to lift a spoon. Not bad for a lady born the daughter of a pauper. Not bad at all.

She ran her hand over her fur jacket, bought two months ahead of the expected winter. Presents. She adored presents. She would make her husband take her somewhere fancy tonight. The old bag could stay with the children. Not like she had anywhere else to go. Not like she had a choice. Zohra giggled as she recalled how she had hit her.

IMTIYAAZ SETTLED INTO A ROUTINE quickly. He would rise early and sit at Halimah's bedside, before helping with chores around the house. His cousins adored him, and he earnestly awaited their arrival from school. He would assist with homework where he could, and then they would play cricket outside until sunset. Aaminah noted his intelligence and she felt helpless. He deserved to go to school.

She had had lengthy discussions with her husband about how best to proceed. Imtiyaaz was on a visit, and they needed to do what they could to transform the visit into a permanent residency. They had met with a solicitor late one evening and he had pointed out the difficulties, granted that Imtiyaaz had a father, his natural guardian. Aaminah spent her nights in an anxious flurry. She needed help and perhaps Bonny was the only one who could assist.

ABOO REMOVED HIS GLASSES TO rub his eyes. He was exhausted. He had been alerted to the fact that Imtiyaaz had left his father for Bonny and, as a trustee, he knew he had to intervene. He drove to Hoosen, an excruciatingly long journey, but a necessary one. He had heard disturbing stories from both Hoosen and Zohra about how Imtiyaaz had chosen to treat his stepmother. Zohra had gracefully accepted the poor treatment and she had been so concerned about him leaving home. Hoosen too was distraught. Both Hoosen and Zohra had wept incessantly, and they had kept him up the entire night with the accounts of Imtiyaaz's behaviour. Aboo felt himself doubting his friend's assessment of his son and daughter-in-law. They appeared to be good people. Imtiyaaz had obviously been spoilt by his grandfather and had now taken to ruling in the home.

Aasiyah had aged considerably, and Zohra had advised that Aasiyah preferred not to be disturbed. Aboo had tried to have a moment with her, to reminisce about old times when they used to all visit the dam every second weekend to spend family time, but he was careful not to disturb her. Zohra was the only one who went in and out of the room as apparently Zohra was the only one with whom Aasiyah felt comfortable.

"What an exceptional daughter-in-law you are," Aboo mused.

Zohra smiled. "I love this family. It's such a pity what we are going through," Zohra said.

"It is," Aboo agreed.

"Hoosen has taken it quite hard. He tries. We both do. I see he is considering removing Imtiyaaz from the line of inheritance," Zohra said, testing the waters.

Aboo did not conceal the shock on his face.

"That is drastic. I don't think it needs to be taken to that extent. The boy just needs to be brought back and be taught who is in charge. Family problems happen. We don't deprive people of inheritance because of it," Aboo said.

Zohra could feel that she had gone too far.

"Don't discuss it with Hoosen. I don't want him to think that I am stirring up more trouble," Zohra said, slowly.

"Not to worry. He probably said that in anger. He can change nothing without the trustees," Aboo said, reassuringly. Aboo thought that Zohra was so kind to be concerned about Imtiyaaz's financial well-being.

Zohra felt bitterness rise to her throat. This wasn't in Hoosen's hands. She needed to find alternative means to sway the trustees to get things to go her way. This was more complicated than she had anticipated.

"I'm glad you could come," Zohra said, mustering a smile.

"Not to worry. I have this under control. Imtiyaaz will be home and things will settle in no time," Aboo said.

He excused himself before heading into the backyard to read the newspaper, completely ignorant of the hisses flying Aasiyah's way.

BONNY FLUNG HIS ARMS UP in exasperation.

"This is unbelievable! I saw the boy soon after it happened! Now you want me to believe some utter nonsense about my grandson!" Bonny yelled.

"I spoke to the treating doctor," Aboo repeated.

"So what? He is probably a buy-out," Bonny responded.

"A buy-out? Are you listening to yourself? A doctor wouldn't place his entire profession under threat," Aboo said, groaning inwardly.

"We cannot force him to go back. Omar will not rule over me from his grave. Goodness knows, I gave in too easily when I put in the adoption bid," Bonny said, scathingly.

"Is that what this is about? Your ego?" Aboo asked, his gaze penetrating.

Bonny drenched the room in his sarcastic laugh. "My grandson was physically violated, emotionally abused and, on top of it all, he was forced to leave school! It is unthinkable that as a trustee you don't see that he needs to be assisted," Bonny said, his voice suddenly calm.

"I am acting in his interests. You do know that Omar left the bulk of the estate to him. He must go back and claim his place," Aboo said.

Bonny fell silent. It was a huge estate, and he did want his grandson to be financially stable. "Then he cannot live with Zohra," Bonny said, firmly.

"That's his home. Don't interfere," Aboo warned.

"He cannot be abused!" Bonny shouted, his anger escalating once more.

"Well, it doesn't seem like he is being abused. He will be coming home. Don't make me press charges for kidnapping," Aboo threatened.

"What are you talking about? I am not afraid of your charges! The boy came to me, abused, seeking help!" Bonny yelled.

"You funded his travels abroad. Wonder how you got that right with the papers?" Aboo questioned, his voice now sarcastic.

Bonny drew his breath in.

"You know what you need to do," Aboo said, his job done.

"I am not afraid of you. I won't do it," Bonny said, firmly.

Aboo walked out of Bonny's house, slamming the door behind him. He was aware that this time the threat wouldn't work. He might have to fly to Europe. Aboo rolled his eyes. He earned a considerable amount as a trustee and Omar had been dear to him, but this seemed a bit excessive. He sighed. Well, he could consider it a vacation so it wouldn't hurt to travel and, of course, he would return with the boy.

"Why do you make life so difficult for Mom and Dad?" Salma asked Hamza.

Hamza lowered his head.

Salma had taken on a great deal in life. She was fully responsible for caring for an elderly lady at the family home where she boarded. She assisted with baking, washing meat, doing the dishes, bathing children and, of course, attending both school and madressah. She had no time to interact with girls her age, save for an hour on Saturday and one on Sunday, when she borrowed the bike of a neighbour to give reign to her athletic nature. Salma, however, did not sink to the level of complaining. She knew that this was the price she needed to pay for her meals, a roof over her head, and the ability to go to school.

The family was kind to her, in the way that they knew how. This was just the way of the world and she found that she loved the children in the home. They took her in as a sibling, as she did them, despite her being slightly older. The head of the family home, a tall man in his mid-forties, treated her as he did his own children. He purchased her clothes when he did for his own, even though that wasn't often. He spoke to her gently and had once even cut her fringe. He noted how responsible she was around the home and, even though she was young, she would need to learn, just the way his daughter Zubeida needed to.

"Ignore me," Salma continued.

Hamza did just that.

"Try to behave! Stop running out of boarding houses. Causing problems," Salma yelled.

"Mind your manners. Please remember that I took care of you!"
Hamza shouted.

"Yes! You cut my nails. You covered my books and saved your
spending money to put stickers on them. You combed my hair. You,
you, made sure I got to eat at school, and you bought me toys," Salma
said, now crying. "This matters to me because you matter to me,"
Salma continued. "Think of Ma. Think of the stress. You know how
Dad is. He gets angry! They are so poor. They did their best for us. Try
and honour them through how you act. It's their name you are carrying
around in town," Salma said, her tears pooling.

Hamza remained silent. A chord had been struck. He stepped out of
the garden at Salma's boarding house, and she watched him walk all
the way down the street. She patted at her tears and tightened the elastic
around her ponytail. She still had lunch dishes to finish.

"MAKE ME *MAAF*. MAKE ME *maaf*," came a quiet voice.

Imtiyaaz sat up immediately and grasped Halimah's hand.

"Mama, Mama, are you okay?" he asked.

"Make me *maaf* for not protecting you," she said, breathing heavily.

Imtiyaaz was unsure of whether this was directed at him or if
Halimah was speaking from her place of understanding; the place
where she continuously sought peace; the place where she spoke to
Khadeejah.

"I heard it. What you said about your father and Zohra," Halimah
said.

"When, Mama?" Imtiyaaz asked, alarmed that he had spoken words
that upset her but also astonished that she had heard and was openly
communicating.

"My accident. It made me a child. A dependent. I float in and out.
Not easy. Not easy to be a dependent," she said.

"Mama, Khala loves you. We all do," Imtiyaaz said, speaking
loudly. He hoped that Khala would hear him so that she could talk to
Halimah.

"Make me *maaf*, my most beloved. I love you. Make me *maaf* that I can't get to my feet to protect you," Halimah repeated.

"Mama, Mama, I can't make you *maaf* when you did nothing wrong," Imtiyaaz cried.

"*Maaf*, my boy," Halimah said, before slipping into her safe place. Her place of solitude. Her place free of pain.

Imtiyaaz was bounding down the stairs to tell Aaminah about what had transpired when he saw her and Uncle standing in the entrance hall with none other than Aboo.

"Imtiyaaz! Nice to see you!" Aboo exclaimed.

Imtiyaaz's heart thudded in his chest.

"Aboo Bhai. Let's discuss this," Uncle said, glancing sadly at his wife and Imtiyaaz.

He had known that Imtiyaaz's paternal family would not let him live in peace, but he had hoped to try to get Imtiyaaz rights before a representative arrived. It had been a futile hope.

"Nothing to discuss. The boy has had his fun. You had your family reunion. It's done. Time for him to go home," Aboo said, emphasising his words.

"Never," came Aaminah's voice.

"Don't challenge me on this!" Aboo threatened.

He dropped a folder to the floor. "Find in there a medical report, a list of charges that I can institute against your father and, above all, the financials which prove Imtiyaaz doesn't work as hard as he says he does," Aboo said, coolly.

"I believe my nephew. He told me about the doctor's lies. Even if the financials are true, he is a boy! His father needs to step up and work!" Aaminah said.

"I stand by my wife and nephew," Uncle said.

"I will press charges against Bonny and you!" Aboo yelled.

Imtiyaaz felt his head spin. Charges? He couldn't let that happen.

"Do what you wish!" Uncle said, stepping forward.

"You have 48 hours. Forty-eight hours," Aboo said, before leaving.

The household was in a shambles and Imtiyaaz saw the strain, the tears, the worry. They spoke endlessly about the way forward and Uncle promised Khala that he would use every shilling to protect their nephew. Imtiyaaz felt the guilt rise. He walked into Halimah's room at a little after 2AM and gently took her hand.

"Mama, I love you," he whispered.

He thought of her words the previous morning, as if she had known that Aboo was downstairs. It made sense. That was love. A love strong enough to anticipate. A love strong enough to know. A love that had kept him alive all these years.

"I am okay, Mama. Don't worry about me," he said, his words catching in his throat. "We will meet again. I promise," Imtiyaaz said.

Imtiyaaz let himself out of the house and walked aimlessly. He could go back and face his life. He couldn't let other people suffer because of him. Or, he could go to Aguutar and convince his grandmother, Omar's other living wife, of the situation. She could assist. She was in her senses. Or he could stay here and fight. No, no, no: he couldn't. Khala, Mama, Uncle and Bonny Papa had too much to lose. He would have to leave them out of it. He would need to ease their pain as well. Even if he had to lie. He drew his breath in. Would lying hurt them more? But would it not save them anxiety?

Imtiyaaz didn't notice the sun rise hours later. He lay listlessly on a park bench. He knew what he had to do. He walked into a pawn shop and undid his watch. It was a Raymond Weil, a gift from Omar. He was probably too young to own one, anyway. He accepted the money. Imtiyaaz let himself back into the house.

"Khala. Uncle. I want to go back," he announced.

Aaminah glared at him, horrified.

"I think I over exaggerated. I think I was too sensitive. That is my father at the end of the day. I must go back," Imtiyaaz said.

Aaminah dropped her tea towel to the table. "Are you worried about the problems?" she asked, her voice barely audible.

"No," Imtiyaaz lied. "I just don't want all of you to go through all the trouble when deep down I know I still have a responsibility to my father. My living parent," Imtiyaaz said, knowing his words had the ability to destroy.

"Why do this then?" Aaminah shouted.

"I have come to my senses," Imtiyaaz answered.

Two hours later he was at the airport; not back to Africa but with the untold intention of going to Aguutar. This was his only hope. He blocked his aunt from his mind. It had been necessary. He had to protect them as they had protected him.

IMTIYAAZ SPUN AROUND AS HE felt a finger tap his shoulder.

"I see you are ready to leave," Aboo snarled. He had expected the boy to be at the airport. Predictable.

"Enough already!" Imtiyaaz screamed.

"Enough? We haven't even begun. You need to stop being a spoilt brat and start taking control of your life! Have you forgotten who you are? Who your grandfather was? The responsibility he trusted *you* with? Have you no shame that I had to travel halfway across the world to hunt you down and take you back home? And what of your Grandfather Bonny? Do you realise the strain you have put him under with your lies? Your grandmothers? Your aunt? You used them because your whole life you could not accept that your father has moved on. Get with it! Yes, your mother died, and yes, it is devastating, but you have a kind and gentle stepmother who has done so much to try and win you over. She has been in tears since you left. She blames herself!" Aboo screamed, attracting the attention of passers-by with his angry speech.

Imtiyaaz felt the familiar disbelief and anger swallow him. How was it that the victim was seen as the oppressor? How did Zohra manage to draw a veil over the eyes of most? His biggest offence seemed to have been breathing, and he had tried multiple times to win her over. She had rejected him, framed him, oppressed him, and yet she still emerged victorious? The court of life had failed him, dismally. He then thought of Bonny, Khala and his beloved grandmother. He had sought shelter with them, without realising the damage it may cause. He had sacrificed their respect for him for their own safety and happiness. That's who he was. He felt himself slipping into numbness. A numbness that occupied his every breath until, a few days later, his feet stopped outside his father's home. His return was acknowledged only by harsher treatment: with spite; with hatred.

The days, weeks and months merged into a seamless darkness. Imtiyaaz watched Aasiyah wither away. He was given quarters close to the back of the house. He was not permitted to enter the kitchen, so he ate his meals, cooked with or by the domestic, outside. A day of baked beans, a day of tinned spaghetti. His skin darkened with the exposure to the severe sunlight, for he was not to enter the house unnecessarily and he walked to and back from the shop whilst his father drove his other children to school and back. His menial earnings were kept in a shoe box at the shop, and he was to explain his spending, down to that spent on shoe polish. He was desperate to be saved but he wasn't sure who could save him. There was no hope. No butterfly to bamba.

Salma waited patiently until the door to the outdoor bathroom opened. There were very few homes in the area that had bathrooms attached to the house, but it proved to be quite an impediment in this household as Sakina Nani struggled to get to the bathroom and back. She was in her late eighties, suffered from diabetes, and had lost two children whose funerals she hadn't been informed of as her living children feared the toll on her health. She was often confused and would insist that Salma assist her with packing her suitcase, as she needed to go back to 'Kliptown township' to see to her husband and young children. Salma, in those instances, would try and indulge her until she forgot about her request, which would sometimes be a few minutes later. Salma sympathised with her situation and would, at times, be late for school because she was seeing to Nani.

"You will tell them that you were helping an old, lost lady come back into the house," Sakina Nani said as her frail figure stepped slowly outside of the bathroom. Sakina Nani, as old as she was, would not accept assistance in the bathroom when needing to relieve herself. She would, however, be bathed by Salma.

Salma clutched her arm and they walked towards the house, Salma assuring her that there was no need to worry about her being late for school. This, of course, was not the case. She would be met with steely gazes from her teacher, who would cruelly tease her about "farm girl time".

Salma, however, excelled in history and English, and her other subjects were placed at comfortable Bs and early As, so her teacher had very little room to cause problems other than emotional disturbances. She struggled only with math, and she would judge herself harshly for this. In any event, she was an athletic asset to the school, she was a delight in home economics, in which she was a finalist in multiple baking competitions. She hoped to be a nurse after school and planned on starting first aid classes after winter. She still had to broach the topic with the boarding family but, as it was after supper dishes would be washed, she couldn't imagine that it would cause too much of a problem.

Hawa, related to the boarding family, would be coming to stay for a few weeks, much to Salma's delight. She hadn't seen Hamza since the interaction in the garden and, even though she had kept an ear out in and about town, she hadn't heard of him causing any trouble. She was glad that he had paid heed to her words.

Hawa arrived at about 11 on a Saturday and Salma had just finished baking a batch of coconut biscuits. She clung to her mother, a paragon of *sabr*. Salma often worried about her mother's condition, in relation to both poverty and her marriage. Hawa had endured her fate and lived only for her children. She knew no other life and only hoped that her children would never have to walk a similar path as adults. Salma had seen the exhaustion hidden in her mother's smile and it pained her greatly.

"Mama," Salma said, finally letting go.

"*Dikra*," Hawa said, using a term of endearment.

"I missed you. Are you okay?" Salma asked.

"I am. Look at how much taller you are!" Hawa commented, her heart swelling with pride.

Her daughter's soft curls and rosy cheeks brought her such pleasure. She was beautiful, inside and out.

"Did you see Hamza and Saida on your way in?" Salma asked.

"I came straight here, so I didn't see Saida. Hamza? Hamza started working on the farm with your father. Didn't you know that?" Hawa asked, confusion etched on her face.

"I didn't know," Salma said.

She felt a mix of emotions. Hamza had come so far not to finish school. He had thrown any possible future of educating himself further away and had essentially taken the route of being a shopkeeper for another. Yet, he would be earning an income, which would assist their home, and it would be a means of keeping him out of trouble. He hadn't told her, though. Why was that?

"It's been a few weeks; perhaps he didn't want you to worry or miss him," Hawa mused.

"Maybe," Salma said, reaching out to hold her mother's hand.

"Salma," Teacher Pradeep called. Salma gathered her books and headed towards his desk. "It's not often that our Indian girls return to school after Standard 8," Teacher Pradeep said.

Salma nodded. Saida had left school at the close of Standard 8 and Hamza had been working in a shop for some years now. Saida too had started working. It had caused a major relief for Rashid and Hawa financially, but Rashid continued to work at the farm shop. They had managed to draw the stoep into the house and had purchased a black couch. Electricity cable drums, circular in nature, had been transformed into makeshift garden furniture.

The farm shop, however, was experiencing dwindling sales and profits were low, so Rashid knew that he would need to make a move. He had discussed it with Hamza, who had been offered a job by the Varachia family in Johannesburg itself. Rashid also knew that his daughters would need to marry as well and, with them living on the farm, their chances of settling would be limited. The farm had become their home and Rashid knew that he would miss it. It was a move, however, which needed to be made.

"I want you to come back to school," Teacher Pradeep said. "You have the potential to finish. You have the potential to study something."

"I want to study," Salma affirmed.

"Good," Teacher Pradeep said as he waved her off.

IMTIYAAZ DISHED OUT A HELPING of creamy potatoes to accompany his roast chicken. The kitchen was warm, and he felt at peace. His friend Abdul and his wife Ariffa teased him about how he had refused to kill any animals on the hunting trip they had just gone on. It had been his first. Imtiyaaz had dinner with Abdul and his wife every evening. It was such a relief to escape his father's house and he had now reached a healthy weight.

Zohra had tried to ruin his friendship with Abdul by trying to befriend Ariffa to fill her head with lies. Ariffa and Abdul, however, knew better, and had put Zohra in her place. This had angered her hugely and she had on numerous occasions locked him out of the house. Two of Zohra's sons had moved to Johannesburg to school, which was convenient for her as they lived with her sister, but this left her with more time to cause havoc.

"You will soon be old enough to marry," Ariffa said.

"It would be a welcome escape," Imtiyaaz answered.

"Marry for the right reasons," Abdul advised.

"I don't know what the issue is with your father, though. He couldn't even stand up for his own mother," Ariffa commented.

Aasiyah had passed away, silently in her bed, and it had been Imtiyaaz who had discovered her. She had suffered along with Imtiyaaz and, although he had been saddened by her death, he knew that she was better off. Bonny too had passed and Imtiyaaz had been overcome by a depression following his death. He knew that he didn't really have anyone on this side of the continent left, and his contact with Khala and Halimah Mama had not been re-established since he'd last seen them. Halimah had just nodded when becoming aware of Bonny's death as in reality he had left her lifeless, a long time ago. Aaminah had wept not for him but for what could have been. Those tears had since dried, and she focused only on her family and her mother.

"I've given up on my father. As a child, I just wanted him to love me. Now it doesn't matter to me. It is what it is. One day I will have my own home and be free of the trauma," Imtiyaaz responded.

"One day soon," Abdul said.

"Any idea of when they will pay you out?" Ariffa asked.

"None," Imtiyaaz answered. The conversation then turned to the latest property developments in the area and, before Imtiyaaz knew it, he was asleep on the couch.

"YOU COULD HAVE PURSUED THIS professionally," Advocate Khan commented as he gracefully lost to his tennis opponent.

"Only if you were always my opponent," Imtiyaaz teased, with a huge grin.

"Your father just doesn't see the gold in you," Advocate Khan said, with a deep sigh.

"He just sees the gold I can generate for them," Imtiyaaz said, his mood now sombre.

Advocate Khan patted him on his back. "I didn't say that to upset you. I am just upset with the wasted potential," the advocate said. The specks of grey that decorated his wavy hair glistened in the sunlight.

"I know, but what can I do? Everyone sees the potential except him, and no one has been able to stand up for me, even when his wife abuses me" Imtiyaaz said, his honesty brutal.

"I know. I should have said something. I should still say something. It's just out of respect to your grandfather that I hold my tongue," the advocate admitted.

Imtiyaaz remained silent. Hidden sympathy had no purpose.

Zohra twirled a lock of her hair around her finger. Her youngest sister had reached a marriageable age and, after having noted the comfortable situation that Zohra had secured, her father had asked her to intervene in finding a suitably rich partner – in the name of Imtiyaaz.

"Think of it. You have the father; she has the son. The money will be all for you. Win-win," he said, his eyes twinkling.

Zohra nodded. That was a good idea. She hadn't been able to reach finality on his inheritance and she knew that, should he be married to her sister, she would still have control of the funds and financial security. This was a stroke of sheer genius.

"Consider it done," Zohra said with a determined nod. "Send Yumna to come live with me."

A week later, Zohra knocked on Imtiyaaz's door. She had prepared a breakfast tray for him, her hatred concealed by her greed. Imtiyaaz opened his door and found himself standing across from his arch enemy.

"For you, my son," Zohra said, her voice catching briefly in her throat.

Imtiyaaz stared at her and did not accept the tray.

"I want to patch things up with you. You haven't been the best son, but I want to forgive you," Zohra said.

Imtiyaaz did not move, and Zohra pushed the tray closer to him. Imtiyaaz reluctantly accepted it but had already resolved not to eat the food. The woman could not be trusted. He was, however, keen to understand her behaviour. Could it be that his father had found it in his heart to finally love him and demand good treatment for him?

"Eat, my child. Why don't you stay at home with me today? I will tell Papa to go to the shop. Let's have some quality time," Zohra suggested, plastering a sickly smile on her face.

"I will have, just now. Give me a few minutes," he said, as he walked out of his room towards the bathroom. Her eyes narrowed. He was too smart for her. She needed to simultaneously run Plan B.

YUMNA SWEPT A HAND THROUGH her silky hair and tried to catch Imtiyaaz's eye. Imtiyaaz, however, rolled his eyes inwardly and headed out the back door. He was off to play tennis and wasn't sure what this woman wanted from him. She resembled Zohra but was darker in complexion and had a gold slit on her front tooth. Her voice was high-pitched, and she had not disguised how much she enjoyed material pleasures.

Yumna had eyed Zohra's lifestyle greedily for some time. She could easily grow accustomed to having meals out often, being bought new clothes weekly, and not having to do any chores. It was a far cry from their family home and Yumna was more than ready to marry Imtiyaaz. She had been delighted at the suggestion and had stayed up late on multiple nights, plotting the scheme with her other sisters. They were a family of six sisters, and it was only Zohra who had married into money.

Yumna angrily watched Imtiyaaz depart. "I made fresh pineapple juice. You will enjoy it; especially with this weather," Yumna said, her voice floating into the backyard.

Imtiyaaz did not acknowledge her. Could it be that Zohra had intended Yumna for him? That was the only plausible explanation for her change in behaviour. Well, it would be a wasted effort. "I'd choose death over it," Imtiyaaz murmured..

"MY PRECIOUS HOOSEN," ZOHRA SAID, placing a hand on her fast-ageing husband's shoulder.

"Jee, my beautiful love," he said, turning to look into her eyes. It had been years since he'd married her but his love for her had done nothing but augment.

"I've heard rumours about Imtiyaaz. It seems he is running around town. I am concerned that he will bring the family name into disrepute," she said, drawing up concern in her eyes.

Hoosen's jaw tightened. How much more nonsense did he have to put up with from Imtiyaaz?

"Which rumours? Who was your source?" Hoosen said, rising from his seat.

"Don't worry yourself. I care about you too much to share the details with you. I have a solution for you, though. These rumours have filtered into South Africa as well, and my dad is very concerned. He raised it with Yumna and Yumna is now willing to make a sacrifice for her nieces and nephews. For us. She will marry him to protect our family name. Let me emphasise that this is a huge sacrifice. She has received many proposals, but I explained my fears to her, as well. I thought of my daughters. Imagine if their future in-laws knew that Imtiyaaz ran around! They would be treated badly. But then again, so many people know. They won't marry at all!" Zohra squealed, forcing tears.

Hoosen disregarded that his children, particularly his daughters, were years away from marriage. He wiped away Zohra's tears and thanked her for looking out for the best for their family. He would, however, be bringing hell down upon Imtiyaaz for causing the family name to be dragged through mud.

"You have to promise me something, though. You can't tell him about our discussion or that we know about his cheap antics. He won't agree to the marriage just to spite us. You know how he hates our family," Zohra said, turning on the faucet of fake fresh tears.

Hoosen nodded. Zohra was right. She was always right. How blessed was he to have a wife with such foresight?

"I don't think the plan is working," Yumna whispered to Zohra.

"It will! Just leave it to me. I will have us basking in riches before you know it," Zohra said in a hushed tone.

Zohra led Yumna into the kitchen and sat across from her, whilst Hoosen fried *bhajias* for the second time this week. Hoosen longed for home cooking, but Zohra made meals less and less often, so they had most of their meals out. Hoosen had now befriended an older couple in an impoverished set of flats, and he had suggested purchasing groceries for them in exchange for the elderly wife cooking meals for them. It seemed like a feasible option. He would, however, take care of breakfast and treats for teatime. Yumna had come in and cooked upon her arrival, but those efforts had diminished as Zohra had warned her not to create a habit and expectation.

Zohra had grown up in a home where table manners were not attended to, and she often laughed and spoke with her mouth open. She would also delay bathing and roam the house in a filthy state until it was time to go out. Yumna was no different and Imtiyaaz gagged at her scent each morning when she sauntered past him. This morning was no different and Imtiyaaz had escaped through the back door just before Yumna approached Zohra.

"It's time for you to tell Imtiyaaz that he will marry Yumna," Zohra said, a piece of sweetcorn that had escape from the bhajia decorating her lower lip.

"My son is a failure. Good of you to want to marry him," Hoosen said to Yumna.

"My father looked at my sister's happiness. I could have married very, very well," Yumna said, blinking counterfeit tears. "I have to stand with my family."

Hoosen was touched and, when he returned from town an hour later, he returned with a box of Ferrero Rocher for both Zohra and Yumna.

Hoosen walked into the shop just after two and noted that Imtiyaaz was in an animated discussion with Yusuf, Abdul, and a few younger men from town.

Imtiyaaz's friends felt the uneasiness upon Hoosen's entry and chose to leave the shop, fearing that their extended presence would worsen Hoosen's attitude.

"What did they buy?" Hoosen asked.

"Nothing today," Imtiyaaz said, neatening the counter.

"So, it's a meeting place for you?" Hoosen asked, slamming his hand against the cash register. "They are not housing you; they are not feeding you, and they are not your father! I expect you to work. But you cannot even do that. Don't you worry! There will come a day when you will need this job and not have it!" Hoosen screamed.

Charlotte, who was repacking the shelves, bowed her head and cursed under her breath. Imtiyaaz was a kind soul; he did not need this kind of treatment. She wondered if she could gather the courage to speak on his behalf, but she then thought of the three mouths that she had to feed.

Imtiyaaz held his breath and prepared for all the belittling that was to come.

"Your games will come to an end. I am arranging your marriage to Yumna. If you want to keep the job and have access to money and the inheritance that my father cheated me out of, you will do what I say!" Hoosen shouted.

"I will not do it," Imtiyaaz said, quietly but firmly.

He had caught on to Zohra's intentions but hearing it out loud sickened him to the pit of his stomach. He had accepted a lot; he would not accept this.

"We shall see about that," Hoosen said, his threat hanging over Imtiyaaz momentarily. Imtiyaaz had tried running away before. It had not worked but he was older now; surely, he could be on his own? He would find a job, even with his lack of skills, and he would be free. The inheritance? He was entitled to it but, unlike his father, he was not dependent on it. He could achieve on his own. This perhaps was a blessing in disguise. He would leave as soon as possible.

"Where are you going?" Hoosen asked, his body now shaking with anger.

"You gave me an ultimatum. I do not want to disrespect you – you are my father – but I will not be able to fulfil your command. It's best we part," Imtiyaaz said, graceful and respectful, even now. Imtiyaaz reached out to hand the shop keys over.

"You are going nowhere!" Hoosen screamed.

A small crowd had gathered outside the shop door. Hoosen tossed Imtiyaaz's keys against the tins of baked beans.

Imtiyaaz crouched behind the counter; fearful of causing a scene in front of the gathering crowd. Hoosen glared at them. "You can all see my useless son! Worthless! Failure! Come! Come and see!" Hoosen belted out, inviting the crowd in with his hands.

IMTIYAAZ FOLDED HIS ARMS AND dropped his gaze as his father entered the room. Imtiyaaz had, as a last resort, called a meeting with the trustees. He had faced a gruesome two weeks. Hoosen had ensured that Imtiyaaz was financially stifled so that he could not make any attempts to flee. As an extra precaution, Hoosen had also spread the word around a few neighbouring towns, within an hour's vicinity, that, should Imtiyaaz seek work, they should not hire him. Imtiyaaz had realised this when he was declined by both a clothing store and a Just Bread, which had recently opened in an adjacent town.

Hoosen noted the look of reproach on the faces of the trustees. They had never believed Imtiyaaz before, but this version of events had been confirmed and they were, if nothing else, overcome with disgust.

"Hoosen, I didn't believe that we would ever meet to discuss something like this," a steely voice said.

"I don't see why we have to. Zohra, as a mother, and me, as a father, know that the boy is running around, and Zohra's sister is willing to take on the liability and marry my worthless son! My cheap son!" Hoosen belted.

Imtiyaaz cringed.

"If Zohra is as much of a mother as you say, her sister would be Imtiyaaz's aunt. How is it that you can marry your son off to his aunt?" the voice asked. Aboo shook his head in agreement.

"We have played along with everything because you have always been right, Hoosen. We looked at the legacy your father left. This time, he too, would toss in his grave. This marriage will not take place. Your sister-in-law is to return to Fietas in Joburg, and Imtiyaaz will return to the shop. The boy also needs a car. He needs to be allowed to travel, especially to see his aunts and uncles – here I refer to Bonny's children," the voice ordered.

Hoosen's humiliation quickly translated into hatred. The boy was being chosen over him again. Just the way his father had always done.

"The estate is doing well, in other news. Properties are yielding good returns," Aboo said, trying to slice through the tension. He had seen the anger flare in Hoosen's eyes, and he wasn't prepared for respect to be lost. "Take Zohra away on a holiday. It will ease the, uhm, disappointment," Aboo continued.

"Why will she be disappointed? She was doing me a favour! You don't care that the boy is running around," Hoosen shouted.

"False accusation. I asked," the steely voice said.

Imtiyaaz wondered why they had not checked up on the facts when Zohra had stoned him, as they had this time. What had changed? He thought to ask but then saw the cold gaze of the trustees and thought better of it. He would take his blessing and be content. He had been saved.

"Meeting over," the voice announced. Imtiyaaz tried to thank them but was met with silence, so he walked out gracefully. Hoosen stayed longer, but Imtiyaaz knew that he wouldn't be able to shift their decision. There had been a sense of finality.

Yumna departed the next day, and it was a week later that his father and Zohra were packing their suitcases. Imtiyaaz chuckled when he saw this; his father had obviously tacitly accepted the disappointment after denying it. In any case, peace would arrive with their departure, even if only for a few weeks.

"I AM VERY HAPPY THAT you are returning to school," Rashid said, "you can qualify and do something. You will be the first in our family."

Salma grinned. She was terribly excited that she brought a sense of hope to her parents. Matric was in sight, a rare achievement for an Indian farm girl in apartheid South Africa.

Salma cherished every moment at home, and she spent lots of time helping Hawa pack. The move was imminent, and it was the first time that the family would be moving to a home in a central town. Hamza had found a place with three bedrooms and, even though it required some work, it was far better than any home they had lived in previously. It was a step up and Hamza was grateful that his job and Saida's could take care of most things. Rashid would still need to work, but they could at least live a life that would be hand-to-mouth monthly as opposed to living in abject poverty. Hamza had bought Hawa some new dresses and he waited impatiently for their arrival in Johannesburg.

Salma had been home for the holidays and during this time interest had been expressed in her by a recently qualified doctor. The doctor had studied in Durban, and under the apartheid regime he was quite fortunate. He came from a reputable family that owned a large home in Swartruggens – a quiet town. He would be practising, however, in Johannesburg and wished to settle before starting his promising career in the city.

He had broken his trip at the boarding house a few months ago and had been impressed by the exceptional young lady, whom he later found out was called Salma. Salma was respectable and poised and she had not participated in any form of conversation with him. He valued this trait as it differed greatly from the hordes of girls his mother had introduced him to. They had all been keen to secure him as a husband and had disposed of their bashfulness. Salma was lovely, inside and out, and he was enormously taken by the tart she had made for dessert that evening.

His parents, delighted that he had found a potential bride, had readily contacted Zaytoon to arrange a meeting over tea. Zaytoon had been courteous on the call and had said that she would refer it to Salma's parents.

Zaytoon knew to discuss it with Salma first as she understood that Salma valued her schooling.

"What must we do? Everyone and anyone would jump at this opportunity. Must we tell Rashid and Hawa of the marriage proposal or should we leave it to Salma?" Zaytoon asked, seeking counsel from her husband.

"Or we can allow her parents to make the decision? There is no reason that she should have to choose her path. This is apartheid South Africa, and finding a financially stable husband will hold her in good stead. Her schooling will not," Moosa said.

Zaytoon clicked her tongue.

"Leave it to me," Moosa said, patting his wife's well-rounded arm. He took a bite of a ginger biscuit and motioned for his wife to be quiet. The neighbour was at the kitchen door.

"Having tea already?" a chirpy lady in her mid-fifties asked.

"Jee, come and join us!" Zaytoon said.

"Won't mind if I do!" she said as she took a seat at the kitchen table. Zaytoon poured her a generous amount of tea and handed her a side plate.

"I just got back from the dry cleaners. Zahed has a new thing where he wants his trousers done there! Boys of today; I tell you! He won't even go fetch it himself! Anyway, what can we do? Our children are our children! We will die for them!" Miriam commented.

"That's true. Their happiness comes first," Moosa said.

"These ginger biscuits are so lovely, but just one notch down from Salma's ginger biscuits. I was just telling them at home, Salma bakes the loveliest biscuits! I am absolutely craving her Romany Creams," Miriam gushed.

Zaytoon began to scribble two recipes on a piece of lined cream paper. "Won't be as good as when Salma makes them but try it out," Zaytoon said, sharing two of her prized recipes.

SALMA KNOCKED ON THE DOOR. This was a bitter-sweet moment. She had wept ferociously when she left her mother behind, but she knew that this was for the best. The door was opened nearly five minutes later, and Salma felt discomfort surround her. She hugged the family and shared fruits that she had brought from the farm with her. She walked into her room an hour later and found that the clothing she had left behind had been stacked onto a chair in the corner of the room. Salma wondered if there was a problem, but she wasn't sure how to proceed.

Salma walked out of the room half an hour later with the intention of speaking to Zaytoon.

"What's wrong?" Zaytoon asked innocently.

"Things do feel somewhat different. I hope that you are comfortable with my return?" Salma asked.

Zaytoon began to shed tears. "I don't know how to say this. I know that you are adamant on finishing your schooling, but that isn't the general way of things for Indian girls. I do feel that your pursuit of this is not going to allow you to settle down," Zaytoon said.

"Settle down?" Salma asked.

"Yes. You received a marriage proposal, and I thought that I would discuss it with you first, but I know you wouldn't consider it because of schooling," Zaytoon explained.

"I know it is unfair, but this is the way of the world and Moosa and I feel that we are encouraging you to walk down the incorrect path by hosting you," Zaytoon said.

Salma sank into the depths of the floor. She was a burden. She didn't ever want to be a burden.

The rep who had dropped Salma off would only be passing through again the following week. The environment was frigid, and Salma had wrestled with whether she should go and inform the school that she had chosen not to pursue Matric. She felt that she owed them an explanation, but then again it was her future that had been infringed upon and she would need to accept it without causing a fuss. She had huge levels of *sabr*, a trait inherited from Hawa.

Salma thought of the marriage proposal and what her parents would expect her to do. She didn't want to break any ties that they had with the boarding family; after all, the family had been good to her, and were acting in what they believed to be her interests.

The days dragged by and Salma could liken it only to being dragged across hot coals. The day of departure finally arrived, and Salma drew the zip on her case. She stood up, ironed out the creases of her pants with her palms, and put on a cheery smile.

"Leaving today, already," Zaytoon commented as she saw Salma place her belongings in the entrance hall.

"Jee, the rep should be here by 10 o'clock," Salma answered.

"You must go well. You were a dear member of our family," Zaytoon said.

Salma, rather surprised, took a moment to answer. "Thank you for the opportunity you gave me and the care," Salma said.

The women watched each other silently, in acceptance of the social norms.

"Go well. Give your parents salaams," Zaytoon said.

Salma shook Aunty Zaytoon's hand and she stepped out onto the stoep and sat on a red step. She'd said goodbye to the other children that morning, before they headed to school. She drew her knees up to her chest and gently rocked herself as she awaited the rep's Toyota.

He arrived promptly at 10, and Salma carried her own luggage to the car. He didn't speak much and just wondered why she had bothered coming back when she knew she didn't want to school further. Salma watched the familiar landmarks from the window. The rep didn't pass by the school and Salma was grateful. Her last associated memory of it was happy and she wanted to keep it that way.

Hawa opened the door to see Salma.

"Mama!" Salma smiled, determined to be strong.

"Salma! Why are you here? What happened?" Hawa asked, concern etched over her face.

"I wanted to come home. School isn't what I thought it would be. I am better off here. The school agrees," Salma said, her sentences fragmented.

"Salma, but you chose to go back. You wanted a Matric!" Hawa exclaimed.

"I wanted it, but I don't anymore, Mama. I am home now," Salma said, with a forced smile. She glanced around the kitchen and her heart warmed to see that her mom had an electric stove. As a child, she had cut out a picture in a magazine of a beaming lady standing next to an electric stove. Her mother now had one.

"Is this because of the marriage proposal Zaytoon mentioned?" Hawa asked, thinking of the call Rashid received.

"I don't intend to marry right away. I just want to be home," Salma affirmed.

"We will respect your wish," Hawa said.

Salma turned her attention to the kitchen.

"You have a stove! Oh, Ma, what a journey it has been," Salma squealed with delight.

They had walked a long road, and, despite the circumstances, they were together as a family at last.

That evening they had a warm dinner of roast chicken and Indian vegetables, and Salma recounted her decision confidently. Her family, if surprised, chose to hide it, but they asked her many times if she was confident in her decision. She confirmed that she was. She would find something to do in town, she promised.

"Ma, do you remember that boy Imtiyaaz? Your friend's son? I met him yesterday at the shop. He came to visit his grandmother," Hamza said.

The conversation steered towards Hamza's meeting and Hamza promised to ask Imtiyaaz over for tea. Hawa prayed for him often and would love to see him.

IMTIYAAZ'S FOOTSTEPS WERE SO LIGHT on the parquet floor that one would have vowed that there were only four people in the lounge. It was after 10 and, although he had politely declined the visit to Hamza's house, after promising to come through at a different time, Hamza had insisted.

Hamza had seen Imtiyaaz seated at a corner table, in isolation, at the burger joint adjacent to the garage. Hamza had invited Imtiyaaz to join his slightly larger table, which Imtiyaaz had done. It was after a hefty burger, well-seasoned chips and bottomless Coke that Hamza had asked his friends to come over to his house for coffee and a few games of cards. He had also reminded Imtiyaaz that his mother longed to see him; the son of her dear friend.

Imtiyaaz appreciated the sentiment, as he had before, but he didn't wish to impose late in the evening but Hamza, a vivacious and warm young man, had got him to agree.

Imtiyaaz noted the warmth in the home, and everything was set definitively in its place, from the ornamental brass tea set to the bowl of Quality Street sweets. Hamza's eyes rested on the bowl of sweets, and he reached for a toffee before he passed the bowl around. He thought briefly of the time when they had had no sweets to offer guests, and his heart rejoiced in knowing that their situation had changed somewhat.

"Mama, I have a surprise for you," Hamza said.

Hawa was sipping tea next to the stove. She had now developed arthritis, and the winters were difficult for her. She warmed herself at the stove each night before settling into bed.

"What is it?" Hawa asked.

"Come and see," he said, beckoning her towards the lounge.

Hawa rose slowly and followed Hamza into the lounge. She warmly greeted Reeza and Yusuf, who both saw her as a motherly figure. They often visited her separately for motherly advice and warm roti. Her eyes then moved to the last couch, and she let out a smile of knowing. She was momentarily transported back into time. She saw her friend smiling in the sunlight; she saw her pick apples off a tree; she felt their parting hug.

"My boy, I am so happy to see you," Hawa said, returning to the lounge.

"It's nice to see you too. I remember that you came to see me some years back. I was little then," Imtiyaaz said.

He was incredibly polite and had risen to meet her.

"Your mother was a dear friend of mine. My prayers have always been with you," Hawa said.

Imtiyaaz smiled and thanked her. He always longed to be in the presence of those who had been close to his mother. It kept her alive for him.

"How is your father doing?" Hawa asked.

"He is well," Imtiyaaz answered.

In truth, his father had been placed under the tight hand of a trustee and had had to give in to Imtiyaaz seeing his grandmother in Johannesburg every second weekend. Zohra has been incandescent with rage at the freedom that Imtiyaaz had with a car and that he earned a reasonable salary. He no longer ate at home, so confining him to eating outside of the house had no impact. She had become consumed with finding new ways to cause him pain, but this seemed harder to do with the trustee checking in often. She had begun to think of ways to end the trustee's control or life, but she knew that she could win this only with sweetness. An act needed to be employed, even if it were from a disgraced actress.

Hawa chatted some more before excusing herself. She offered to make tea, but Hamza said that they would have coffee after a game of cards. Hawa reminded him of where to find the freshly baked scones.

"Salma, please make some coffee!" came Hamza's voice down the passageway.

Salma was perhaps on her third dream of the night. She had found a job in a local wool centre and had an early start to the day.

Salma shrugged off his voice and turned over.

Hamza knocked on her door. "Salma, please make coffee for my friends," Hamza said, peeping through the slightly ajar door.

"I'm sleeping!" Salma shouted. Her alarm clock read 23h30.

Imtiyaaz heard her response travel through the lounge.

She turned to face her brother who was now teasing her.

"How many?" she asked.

"Four. And with me, five," he said sheepishly.

Salma rose and put her gown on before walking into the kitchen. Salma put on a pot of coffee and placed mugs and side plates into a tray. She retreated into the passage. Imtiyaaz caught a glance of her rosy cheeks and soft curls. He knew immediately. This was his wife.

Two trustees arrived at Hawa and Rashid's home a month later with a proposal.

Salma was beautiful and intelligent. She was a jack of all trades and could do anything from household repairs to baking outstanding treats. She had always held her dignity with her and had never engaged with the opposite gender, except during school races where she had been the only girl selected to run in boy's races. She was an athlete, and her potential far exceeded the life given to her by the political regime. She was grateful for her religion and her race, but had she been a "white" girl she would have been acknowledged and would have been able to excel, academically and in sport. It would never have been the case that she would have needed to board to school, and she would have had opportunities available to her.

Her mother had shared with her the news that two men would be coming to represent Imtiyaaz with a proposal, and she had remained expressionless. She knew that marriage would eventually be her path, and she could not continue with her entry-level role at the wool centre, despite her initial choice.

Salma went about her life and work and appeared briefly for the period that the trustees were at her house. The trustees spoke with Rashid, assured him that Imtiyaaz was running a business and would someday inherit an empire, that he was a gentleman and that they would be delighted to have Salma join the family. They had done their research on her and felt that she would be a good fit. Hawa's good character was spoken about, so it was evident that Salma would follow suit.

There was no mention made of the difficulties imposed on Imtiyaaz, but the trustees had taken care to ensure that the couple would have their own apartment. Rashid thanked them for their time and said that he would need time to consider the proposal and confirmed that he would let them know either way.

Rashid knew that Salma had grown up in difficult circumstances and, while it would be nice to know that she was taken care of financially, that was not a deciding factor for him. He sought only happiness for his daughter. Hawa praised Imtiyaaz and spoke about the beautiful qualities entrenched in his mother. She told Rashid of her prayer when she had heard of her friend's passing, where their children would marry and, by no physical intention or search, the opportunity had arisen.

Salma listened in silence but was concerned about having to move so far away; to a land unknown to her. She didn't voice her concerns as she trusted her parents' judgement.

"What of his stepmother?" Rashid asked.

Hawa shared what little she knew with the intention only of informing her husband so he could decide, but there had been nothing of concern that she was currently aware of. It was not her habit to discuss people in any case; this was a trait that separated her from the crowd. She saw the best in people and perhaps she was deceived in some instances by people, but she knew that the world was a passing thing, and she didn't wish to get bogged down by trivialities.

Rashid discussed the matter with his wife and son at length before asking Salma if she would be happy.

Salma once more confirmed that she was happy with whatever their choice was.

It was in the next month that Rashid agreed for the family to come up for the proposal to be accepted. Hamza saw to it that he purchased Salma a beautiful dress and she needed nothing more than a slight lip colour to accentuate her features. Saida was fully supportive, and she longed only for Salma's happiness. They would all miss Salma, though. She truly was the warmth of the home, and it had been for such a short time that they had lived as a family.

Imtiyaaz patiently awaited the answer, and his heart leapt when he was told that they would visit her home so that the marriage proposal could be accepted. He wondered what Zohra had planned, as she had been very supportive of the idea and had treated him in a strangely kind way. Imtiyaaz didn't give a lot of himself, but he remained civil.

"Here you go," Mrs Patel said, handing her a suit pack and returning her smile.

Salma politely thanked the greying lady and motioned to her cat to follow her out. Ginger was a stray that Salma had adopted and trained and the two had become inseparable. Ginger accompanied Salma on her errands and spent the afternoons asleep on the rug in the lounge.

"You must give us your cat when you leave," Mrs Patel reminded Salma.

"I will, but it will be so difficult!" Salma expressed.

"Pets are special, but don't worry; she will be in good hands," Mrs Patel said.

This was the weekly exchange that the women shared.

Salma's marriage date was set for two years' time and of those two years just seven months had passed. Salma cherished every moment she had at home. Hamza had insisted that Salma stop working and both he and Rashid provided her with reasonable amounts monthly to purchase items for her trousseau. Salma had a decent but extremely stylish fashion sense, and she purchased items carefully.

Initially, Imtiyaaz had come for visits, but these were kept respectful and Imtiyaaz spoke only to her parents and Hamza. Hamza was fond of Imtiyaaz, and he was grateful that his sister would be married to a man of character. The visits, however, had fizzled out and for the past two months there had been no attempt at any telephonic conversation.

Rashid had grown anxious, as he had been repeatedly asked by neighbours why there was a such a delay in Salma's marriage taking place. An alternative proposal had arisen, and Rashid had demanded that they consider it, granted that there was a complete break in contact between the families. Hawa pleaded with him to turn it down, as she believed that Imtiyaaz would resurface, and that the family was too respectable to just disappear. She was nonetheless concerned, but she kept her faith strong. Destiny was something that would unveil itself in time.

Hamza had left it for his parents to decide but he still believed that Imtiyaaz was a match; something that he aired often.

Imtiyaaz, on the other hand, had been kept busy on the home front. Zohra had done a complete turnaround and was acting graciously in preparation for the wedding and for his new life. He'd also acquired a few properties to place on rental and the trustees and his father felt the significant increase in funds. His father gave him the niceties and he and Zohra revelled in the benefits. Imtiyaaz felt himself leaning towards both her and his father and he was all too reluctant to reach out to Salma's family, on the advice of the trustees. They needed to keep firm and not overextend themselves and Imtiyaaz, as always, accepted their will. Zohra had encouraged less contact with the family so as to maintain respect, and Imtiyaaz, hungry for the care of a mother that had evaded him his entire life, acceded to her will.

Salma coughed nervously. This was her first flight, and she watched as Imtiyaaz paged through a travel guide. He had tried to make her comfortable without embarrassing her and she had been gracious, despite her anxiety. She tried to control her cough and sipped on some water. It helped and she closed her eyes, remembering all that had been and wondering about all that was to come.

It had been two days since their wedding, after a two-year wait. The trustees had become aware that there was much interest in Salma from other families, affluent families at that, and they had, despite the months of silence which had preceded, ensured that contact was initiated and maintained for the better part of the last year.

The family had not questioned Imtiyaaz's disappearance when he'd arrived for a visit on a summer's evening and did nothing more than make him feel welcome. Imtiyaaz connected well with Hawa, and he spent hours talking to her about Aguutar. He noted that Rashid had a slight temper, and he quickly picked up on the dynamic, though he said nothing about it.

The last month prior to the wedding had been a whirlwind, with multiple family members at Salma's house assisting with the preparation of *mithais* and biscuits, as well as with marinades for the anticipated wedding week. There was much warmth and laughter and both crowds and assistance were attracted by Hawa's hospitality and loving nature. Hawa would miss Salma enormously; she had barely had her with her growing up and now it was time for Salma to leave. Hawa tried to brush the thought away as she understood this to be the way of the world, and she did conceal the sadness from Salma. She wanted Salma to leave on a happy and confident note, as nothing would give her greater peace than knowing her daughter had a better life ahead of her. Hawa threw herself into the preparations and made the week memorable. The wedding itself was beautiful; the kind of beauty that emanates from purity and goodness.

Salma's parting was tearful, but Imtiyaaz had tried to console her. His family in Europe had not been included nor invited to the wedding, but this was something Imtiyaaz had no control over, but he imagined how proud Halimah and Aaminah would have been.

The news of his engagement had reached Aaminah, and she had immediately sent an offer to assist. Imtiyaaz was not made aware, and Aaminah waited for a response. Her patience was tested once more when she received no invitation to the wedding of her only nephew. The boy she loved. The boy she had helped raise. Aaminah accepted that they were forgotten to Imtiyaaz, and it re-awoke in her the bad memories of their last parting. It was done and he was gone.

Aaminah hated herself for trying so hard, only to be rejected, time and time again. She didn't mention the marriage to Halimah in their "chats", where Aaminah would detail her daily experiences whilst Halimah silently watched. Aaminah knew her mother heard everything; despite not speaking and she didn't want to inflict any kind of pain.

"A change in lifestyle will be necessary," Dr Mosam instructed. Salma stared at her feet. "You cannot put yourself at risk of a stroke. In one year, I have seen you being diagnosed with high blood pressure, then you picked up jaundice, and now this," the doctor continued, somewhat exasperated.

He didn't understand why people with family issues chose to marry and subsequently bring an innocent party into their issues.

Salma and Imtiyaaz had been married for three years and a large portion of it had been grotesque; not because of Imtiyaaz's behaviour but because of that of Zohra and his father. Initially, whilst the wedding guests from Aguutar were still housed in Imtiyaaz's family home, Salma had been asked to cook all meals, which she had done. She had received much praise from the guests and the townspeople had come to know of her charming and gracious behaviour. She was a style icon, and many women tried to adopt her dress sense and hounded her for her recipes. She befriended all her neighbours, and her home was open to one and all.

Four months into this, and a few weeks after the guests had left, Salma had been informed that she was not to come to Zohra's home, as Zohra was not Imtiyaaz's mother. Salma had been astounded and, in her innocence, had left only after she had served the *rasmalai* that she had carefully made the evening before. Zohra despised Salma, for she was everything Zohra was not and Zohra, despite the age gap, tried to mimic Salma's dressing, down to madly searching for items or accessories that Salma wore.

Salma knew that she had inspired women to dress better and take better care of themselves, but Zohra's obsession far exceeded that of anyone else's. If Salma had been seen wearing a belt over a dress, Zohra would don a belt at every opportunity. Zohra, however, also saw opportunity in this, as she could exploit the situation to deprive Imtiyaaz of his share. She consistently told her husband, wives of the trustees, and anyone who would listen, that Salma was a gold-digger, that she had adopted a five-star lifestyle on the estate's strength, and that she would deplete all the money.

The trustees, having noted the neatness of Salma's home, bought into this story and nothing was said when Imtiyaaz's salary was again controlled out of a shoebox, stored in the shop. Imtiyaaz had to account for every note taken and, when their first daughter arrived, this created a strain as he was in trouble each time he purchased nappies or clothing for his daughter.

Salma had never taken from Imtiyaaz and the clothes that people raved about were bought from the money she'd saved and had been given back home. Imtiyaaz would bring news of his father's complaints day in and day out, and Salma felt the tension build within her. She feared for the well-being of her daughter and eventually she spent lengthy periods of time at her home in Johannesburg – both her and her child – under the care of her father and brother. Many believed that she had divorced, but she remained committed to the idea that someday things would improve for and with Imtiyaaz. He was a kind and loving soul, and she wasn't thrilled that she had to leave him for months at a time, but she knew that her daughter needed care, and she couldn't stand to see Imtiyaaz persecuted for trying to care for his family.

Zohra celebrated each time Salma left, and she knew that she would, in time, issue the final order. She would see Imtiyaaz crumble.

"I will do my best to take care," Salma said to the doctor and rose to her feet. Dr Mosam wagged a finger at her and handed her a prescription. Salma had just returned to Imtiyaaz a month ago, as she had noted her father's anxiety about the situation of her being home. She had not disclosed to her family the true reasons, but she felt that they were now catching on, especially amidst the rumours of divorce. She didn't wish to bring any sadness or shame to the family and had sworn to go back to Imtiyaaz and make do. Farzana, their rosy cheeked and plump daughter, was just over 18 months old and Salma would have to hold it together.

Salma had left Farzana with her neighbour, Razina, and she'd decided to stop by at the shop on her way home. Imtiyaaz was marking prices for goods and Salma, in her neat hand, offered to assist. She hadn't mentioned to Imtiyaaz that she had gone to the doctor, and she had sold a few items of clothing to pay for the fee.

Imtiyaaz smiled broadly at his wife. He was grateful for the visit, and he needed help. He handed her tags to note prices.

Imtiyaaz's younger brother entered the shop half an hour later. "Wow, Salma Bhen, you have such nice handwriting!" he exclaimed. He was innocent, and he was fond of Salma.

"Thank you," Salma said, patting his shoulder. "How was your day at school?" she asked.

"It was good. I have a science experiment. Will you help me?" he asked.

He knew that his mother would not assist, and he struggled quite a bit to do things himself.

"Sure! Do you want to have lunch with us and then I can help you?" Salma offered.

The afternoon went off smoothly and there was much laughter.

Zohra was livid when her son returned home late that evening. Luqmaan explained in his childish innocence. It was before eight the next morning that Salma was instructed that she was not to enter the shop. Zohra had additionally strictly instructed her children to stay away from Salma and Imtiyaaz, should they want a roof over their heads. Salma felt her heart break when she received the warning.

"MMA FARZANA," DINEO CALLED OUT. Dineo was a tiny lady in her early thirties, with a flawless mocha complexion. Salma considered Dineo a friend, as she had taught her the local language and had been of enormous assistance to Salma, particularly when caring for Farzana when Salma was ill.

"Yes, dear," Salma answered, not looking up from her chopping board.

"I want to tell you something because it has disturbed me," Dineo said.

Salma put her knife down and turned to face Dineo, concern gripping her face.

"Today, when you went out with Ra Farzana (Imtiyaaz), his father jumped over the gate. He came into the house and was opening cupboards. He even opened your clothes cupboard!" Dineo stated, more aghast as she spoke what had happened out loud.

Imtiyaaz had moved his precious family into a "council" house. It was a small home but had a massive garden area, in hilly surrounds. It wasn't unusual for monkeys and other animals to venture into the grounds, and they had tried to put up fencing, to no avail. Farzana was happier here; she had fallen ill too many times when they'd lived in the flat because of the poor sewerage system in the area.

Salma felt disgust and anger surface. How was it that he could invade her privacy to the extent of going through her closets? To how much lower a standard could this man drop?

"Thanks for telling me," Salma said.

Dineo nodded before dismissing herself for the day.

Salma barely ate that evening and retired to bed just after seven. Farzana picked up on the restlessness, so she slept without much fuss. Farzana was a demanding child, who constantly sought attention and love, so Salma, on this evening, was grateful for the break.

Imtiyaaz didn't ask too many questions. Salma was now a BP patient, and he knew that she had headaches often. Salma ran through the options in her mind. She couldn't do this anymore. She had to leave. This was no way to live. She had swallowed insults, she had been lied about, and she had stopped maintaining friendships because Zohra would take steps to destroy them. She had to conceal her activities, even when she visited her parents, as Zohra had employed a spy in the name of Saida's husband, who provided updates on everything purchased and done whilst in Johannesburg. It was an issue, even if Salma and Imtiyaaz went to the Milky Lane in Hillbrow to have ice cream. Salma was allegedly usurping the estate's money, and this was unfathomable! All money available was accounted for in the cursed

Bata shoe box and Hamza and Rashid were still providing whatever extra they had for Salma and Farzana.

Saida and her husband lived next door to her parents, so it was easy for news to travel to Zohra. She needed more than anything to get everyone to believe that Salma was diminishing funds and that Imtiyaaz could not be trusted with money. She had already swayed her husband to believe her, and Hoosen had come down extremely hard on Imtiyaaz, particularly since he was trying to get a house in his name.

It was difficult to get involved in the government process, but should Hoosen have had it his way, Imtiyaaz would never have been successful in his application for a house. This scheme ran in such a way that insofar as the house was occupied, minimal repayments were made to the state if one could prove that they were tax compliant. After five years, a reasonable sum would need to be paid with occupancy maintained and ownership would be transferred. Imtiyaaz wanted nothing more than to provide for his family, but as he couldn't really do that to the extent that he would have liked to, he saw it fit to try and provide a roof.

It was after 10AM and the sun felt like it was a touch away. Salma clutched Farzana's hand, and she began to walk down the winding road. She had packed a backpack with necessities, and she intended on walking towards the border, an hour's walk from their home. She had made it down three streets before a Mercedes stopped. The window rolled down to reveal Ebrahim, a close friend of Imtiyaaz's. Ebrahim was a fair man, and he had built his wealth through franchises. His wife had unfortunately faced mental issues and was currently hospitalised, leaving him and his parents to tend to his children.

"Where are you going to?" he asked, directly.

Salma hesitated before deciding to carry on walking.

"I can give you a lift?" Ebrahim offered.

"I don't need one, thank you," Salma answered curtly.

"Running away solves no one's problems. Come, it's boiling outside, and the child looks tired. Let me take you home and you can iron this out properly with Imtiyaaz. If you need to part, don't let it be this way," Ebrahim said.

"I didn't say I was running away," Salma stated, her eyes not moving off the gravel in front of her.

"You didn't have to," Ebrahim responded.

Salma sank into her couch an hour later. She had refused the lift but had turned back home. Her soul was beaten. Her mind was aflame, and she begged her thoughts to stop. She had been brought back to this living hell. It wasn't Imtiyaaz that she was trying to escape, though. He had not wronged her. Her child didn't deserve a broken home. Yet there was no end in sight to the trauma; to the ill-treatment from Zohra and Imtiyaaz's so-called father.

"Mama, I am hungry," Farzana announced as she dropped to the side of the couch.

She was clutching a rag doll and Dineo had used blue tissue paper to decorate the braids in her wavy hair. Salma sighed. She had to choose her family, even over her health and sanity. She pushed herself up and headed towards the kitchen.

IMTIYAAZ WAS REPACKING THE THIRD shelf to the right of the counter when Hoosen walked into the shop. The shop had been busy that morning and Imtiyaaz was looking forward to spending a quiet weekend with his family.

Farzana had just turned five and she was such a joy to be around. Imtiyaaz's love for his family grew each day, but he had a constant fear that they would somehow be taken away from him.

He often went to check on whether his wife and daughter were still in the house and were okay, even whilst watching TV in the late evening.

Jumu'a was in about 45 minutes time and Imtiyaaz was surprised that his father had opted to come to the shop. Imtiyaaz greeted his father but, as usual, met a thin-lipped scowl.

"Today when you leave at 12, leave the keys here. There is nothing for you here and I am closing the shop down," Hoosen announced.

He watched in enjoyment as Imtiyaaz's expression changed from a smile to confusion to shock. Hoosen remained silent.

"Papa, what are you saying?" Imtiyaaz asked.

"You are nothing to me. I don't care if you drown in a lake," Hoosen said, spacing out his words for effect.

Imtiyaaz felt himself tremble. His father was kicking him out of the business! What of his family?

Hoosen flung the till open and emptied out the float into his back pockets. He then picked up the black Bata shoe box and counted the money in it before dropping it to the counter. "Take your money and leave!" he shouted.

Imtiyaaz tried to seek an explanation, but there was none. He begged for *maaf*, thinking he had done something to his father, not realising that he had never wronged his father. There was nothing to seek forgiveness for. He tried to return to the shop after *Jumu'a*, but it was closed. He was barred from entering his father's house and so, with a heart carrying an inexplicable weight, Imtiyaaz returned home.

Salma was spinning Farzana around in a new dress that Rashid had bought and the two giggled. Imtiyaaz's eyes stung with tears. He remembered the time his daughter had hidden behind the couch when she saw Hoosen, as she knew that Imtiyaaz always got reprimanded when she wore something new. Imtiyaaz silently crept into his bedroom and lay on the bed. The sunlight had been suddenly replaced with an overlay of clouds and thunder threatened. He heard Dineo close the windows.

"I didn't know that you were here!" Salma exclaimed as she saw Imtiyaaz lying, defeated. "I thought you went to someone for lunch. Let me warm lunch up for you! We waited until after two," Salma said.

"Daddy! Daddy! You are at home!" Farzana squealed with delight.

Imtiyaaz tried to muster a smile.

A frown developed on Salma's face. "Is everything okay?" she asked, walking towards Imtiyaaz.

"I lost my job. My father told me to drown in a lake. I have nothing! What am I going to do! You! Farzana! *Maaf*! I made you beggars!" Imtiyaaz sobbed, as he began to shake uncontrollably.

Salma's chest tightened and she tried to comfort Imtiyaaz.

Farzana began to cry. Salma didn't know who to give her attention to.

Imtiyaaz felt the acid rise in his chest and for the third time that night he stepped out of bed and began to pace in the lounge. Salma hadn't slept a wink, and she followed him out. They spent the next hour repeating similar phrases, fears and recollections. Salma knew that she had to stand strong, as he could easily crumble. She offered to go back home until things settled, but she voiced her concerns about leaving him in a devastated state. She didn't feel comfortable leaving, but she didn't want to impose.

Imtiyaaz felt his insides catch alight. His wife and daughter were the centre of his life. He loved them immensely and he couldn't handle the thought of being away from them for an indefinite period. Previously, when Salma had spent time at her parents' home, he had known that she would return, but now he didn't know if he would find a job and be able to provide at all. Imtiyaaz did not respond to Salma's offer, and he began to tremble uncontrollably. Half an hour passed in this state and Salma feared for Imtiyaaz. Salma sat at Imtiyaaz's side until she heard a toy box topple.

"Farzana is up," Salma said in a hushed tone. "Let's try not to upset her."

Imtiyaaz sat dully in one spot and this time couldn't even be drawn into a smile when the slightly overweight child sat at his feet, surrounded by toy cars. Farzana loved dolls and cars. She had marked Imtiyaaz out as the one she would seek attention from today, but she was struggling to get it. She grew agitated and it wasn't long before Imtiyaaz had to indulge her. The pair played, but not for a second did Imtiyaaz forget his troubles.

Salma buttered two rolls for herself and Imtiyaaz as the tea was brewing. She had to be extra careful with money now. The family sat down to a late breakfast and Farzana asked for more porridge. Salma didn't have the heart to deny her.

"I think I should ask Shakeel Docrat for a job. His supermarket is doing well," Imtiyaaz said, as the thought struck him.

"Will he give you one? Didn't your father lend him start-up capital?" Salma asked.

"He's a good guy and he knows me. He needs a manager. I heard that rumour a few weeks ago," Imtiyaaz responded.

He wondered why he hadn't thought of this yesterday. Excited, Imtiyaaz bid his family goodbye and drove towards the supermarket. Twenty minutes later, Imtiyaaz was sitting across from Shakeel in a crimson office, left of the supermarket entrance. He explained his situation and Shakeel sympathised with him before assuring him that he could have the job. Imtiyaaz dipped into the refreshing waters of relief and agreed to work Monday to Sunday; for 10-hour shifts. Imtiyaaz hurried home to share the news with Salma.

Salma was concerned about the working hours, but she knew that they had no other choice. Imtiyaaz would start on Monday. The rest of the day passed in tranquillity. The family received unexpected guests from a neighbouring town late that evening and, whilst serving coffee, they heard a car hooting. Imtiyaaz peered out of the window to see Shakeel standing outside his vehicle. Astonished, Imtiyaaz let himself out the front door and headed towards the gate.

"Come in," Imtiyaaz invited.

"No, I really can't. I just wanted to let you know that you shouldn't come in. I thought about the decision again and I don't feel it's right to get involved. Your father has done a lot for me," Shakeel stated, matter-of-factly.

Imtiyaaz nodded and thanked Shakeel for letting him know. Imtiyaaz held a brave face until the guests left. He shared the news with Salma, and he began to weep. His entire life had been a struggle, but this was something that he didn't feel equipped to handle. He faced the pits of the unknown, armed with not even a candle.

The telephone rang shortly after 10 on Monday morning and Salma was startled to hear Zohra's voice.

"I just phoned to let you know that I have finally achieved my goal," she said in a cheery tone. Salma did not offer a response; her manners far exceeded those of Zohra's, and she politely ended the call.

"I think I must phone to let the trustees know. They won't agree to this!" Imtiyaaz announced, after Salma shared the contents of the call with him. Salma agreed with him. Surely it couldn't be that they would turn a blind eye to this, especially because they had been pivotal in bringing Imtiyaaz back home after he had fled. Imtiyaaz's calls, however, went unanswered until the close of the following week.

It was late on Friday afternoon when one of the trustees called. Imtiyaaz recounted the occurrence, but the trustee did not sound surprised in the least.

"Imtiyaaz, I think it's best if you go out and learn a new trade. Then we will open a business for you," the trustee said.

"What trade can I learn? I have a family to support," Imtiyaaz responded, fear and desperation creeping into his voice.

"I can't help this time. Your father will run the shop. You must do something else for now," the gruff, aging voice said.

"But my grandfather pulled me out of school. I was in the business. Give me what is mine and I will make a go of things on my own. Please. Please," Imtiyaaz pleaded.

The phone clicked. Imtiyaaz was baffled. This was the same man who had insisted that Imtiyaaz get a car and that he be treated better. Why had there been such a huge change? Imtiyaaz was also confused about what the trustee had said about his father running the shop. His father had said he was closing it. Imtiyaaz drove past the shop the next day and saw the door open, a few customers inside. With a heavy heart he turned back home.

Imtiyaaz combed the streets, in a desperate search for a job. He had very little money left, and he knew he wouldn't be able to afford monthly groceries at the close of the month. They were fortunate that they had live chickens, but even with that, they now only slaughtered once a week. Farzana had named some of the chickens and Salma and Imtiyaaz had been castigated when they slaughtered her "Hamza Mama." They were, however, in desperate times, and they promised to get her a replacement in time. She had cried for the entire afternoon and both Imtiyaaz and Salma were inclined to join her, albeit for different reasons.

Imtiyaaz walked along the main road and the town's only bookkeeper, standing at the door of his office, called out to him. Mr Botha had just got off the phone with a client who had mentioned that he was in search of a manager to run his hotel. The hotel was situated in a neighbouring town, east of them. Mr Botha had promised to keep a look-out, and once his eyes settled on Imtiyaaz he knew that he may have found the right person. Mr Botha was a professional and he didn't care much for social conflict, so he warmly invited Imtiyaaz into the office. Imtiyaaz listened intently to Mr Botha's proposition and Mr Botha promised to put him forward.

Shahid Habib was in his mid-forties. He had an exceptionally beautiful wife, 10 years his junior, as well as two beautiful daughters aged 14 and 10. He had lost his father at a young age and he and his older brother had taken on the responsibility of caring for their mother and sisters. This had earned the brothers great rewards, and the elder brother had made a fortune in the food industry, with his vast financial menu boasting both restaurants and take-aways. He was now expanding his profile by looking at investing in a pharmaceutical company that had a footprint in sub-Saharan Africa.

Shahid had, on the other hand, a smaller portfolio consisting of a shop and a 40-room hotel, but he couldn't keep up with managing the business on his own as it was a full-time commitment that needed a presence for at least 16 hours a day.

Mr Botha, after having met with Imtiyaaz, called Shahid and let him know that there was a man in search of a job, and he was available immediately. Mr Botha opted to stand as a "guarantee" for the man's honesty. Shahid enquired about his employment history but, as Mr Botha was not aware of the true reason why Imtiyaaz was no longer a part of the family business, he provided Hoosen's contact details, as per Shahid's request.

Hoosen answered the telephone on its fourth ring. "*Assalaamu alaikum*, Hoosen. You are speaking to Shahid Habib," came Shahid's voice. He had a firm and powerful voice.

"*Wa alaykum salaam*. Shahid from Presidency?" Hoosen questioned, confused by the call.

"Yes. I have a job opening for a manager and I hear that your son is looking for employment. I want to offer it to him but, before I do, I want you to honestly disclose the reason why he is no longer with you in business," Shahid continued, cutting to the chase.

Hoosen's eyes narrowed, and he cursed.

"I didn't quite hear you," Shahid said, interjecting Hoosen's thoughts.

"Shahid Bhai, don't make the mistake I made. My son is a failure. You will regret it if you hire him! He did me down, such... a failure!" Hoosen said, pausing for effect.

"Thank you, Hoosen. That's all I needed," Shahid said before placing the receiver on its base. Shahid was a phenomenal judge of character, and he was grateful he'd made the call.

He dialled Mr Botha ten minutes later. "Mr Botha, it's Shahid," Shahid said in a business-like tone.

"Yes?" Mr Botha responded, mentally preparing himself for how to break more bad news to Imtiyaaz.

"I spoke to his father. He says the boy is a failure. Bring that failure to me; he's just who I need," Shahid said.

Mr Botha smiled into the receiver. "I will tell him to come see you," Mr Botha said.

"Send him to my house, tomorrow night. With his family," Shahid instructed.

"Done," Mr Botha said.

Farzana's eyelids drooped and her head fell against Salma. They were seated in a cream lounge, at the Habib residence. Their lounge was large with intricate ornaments gracing marble coffee tabletops. Mehroon Habib was a gracious woman, characterised by luscious hair and well-defined brows. Her daughters Raadia and Rubina were friendly, and they had entertained Farzana until her bedtime kicked in. Mr Habib's soul had been touched by Imtiyaaz's innocence, at the unity of their little family, and by the lack of greed. Imtiyaaz was willing to accept the job on any terms and he hadn't asked any questions surrounding pay or benefits until Shahid mentioned it. The job came with a company house, free petrol and a salary that was 20% higher than what Imtiyaaz had earned working at the shop.

"Come and see the house tomorrow. I haven't been there myself in some time so I can't speak to the condition," Shahid said.

"Not to worry," Imtiyaaz answered. He was just grateful for the job, and it was of huge assistance that he wouldn't be required to pay rental. The families parted, but Salma was quiet on the drive home.

Farzana slept soundly on the back seat.

"What's wrong?" Imtiyaaz asked.

"I think you should test the job for a few months before we all move up as a family," Salma said.

Imtiyaaz nodded in agreement. He had no experience in this industry, and he wasn't sure if he would be competent or kept on should he stumble in the beginning. His excitement turned into self-doubt.

Salma read his mind. "I don't think that you are incapable. You have a lot to offer. You just need to familiarise yourself with things. Start at ground level and learn everything, even from the person with the smallest role. I am just worried that you won't like the job and that you are leaving the town you grew up in," she said, airing her thoughts.

Imtiyaaz shared his fears with her, and she reassured him that, should it not work out, they would find something else.

As agreed, the family met Mr Habib outside the address of the company house at 11 the next day. It was five minutes away from the business, but it was situated on a sand road. Salma's eyes widened at the length of the weeds, which far exceeded Farzana's height. The grounds were clearly unkempt. Imtiyaaz lifted his daughter, and they walked towards the front door. It was wooden, with yellow-stained panelled glass both to the right and left.

The key turned in the door and nothing could have prepared them for the stench that met them. The house smelt of urine and the paint had chipped off the walls in the entrance hall. It was a three-bedroom house with a narrow passageway. A fourth room, adjacent to the lounge, had dilapidated shelving, but the lounge and dining room were of a decent size. The veranda had scratched tiles and no form of burglar bars, despite it overlooking a maze of weeds and a short boundary wall.

The family remained silent throughout the tour and retreated to the car with the house keys now in their possession. They thanked Mr Habib politely and did not display their shock.

"Dineo will have to come with you to clean the house. Maybe Shortie can help with the weeds," Salma said, planning the course of action.

"Will you be okay without me and Dineo?" Imtiyaaz asked.

"I will. I want you to settle in," Salma said.

The weekend flew by in trying to eradicate grime and weeds, but by sunset on Sunday there was still much that had to be done. Imtiyaaz had, with Salma urging him to, used most of his remaining money to buy a bed.

"We can always sell it if this doesn't work out," Salma said, her voice always staying confident and encouraging.

Imtiyaaz teared up as he said goodbye to his family that evening. Tomorrow would be a huge day for him, and he wouldn't have them with him. Imtiyaaz couldn't sleep a wink, and neither could Dineo and Shortie. Shortie had once worked at the shop and now did ad hoc gardening jobs. The house was foreign, and they could all have sworn that they heard the toilet flush on its own; not surprising as the house had been uninhabited for some time.

The trio shared a loaf of bread and water for breakfast the next morning as they had no fridge, and the stove didn't seem to work. Imtiyaaz, however, put on a positive attitude and stepped into the hotel for the first time. His day was spent with introductions and a tour. He had a tiny office with a wooden desk and blue chair. Imtiyaaz greeted the staff warmly and made sure he remembered their names. Imtiyaaz, when analysing the day's events that evening, realised that this was a demanding space and once more he wondered if he could make a go of it.

"I have to for my family. I need to," he affirmed numerous times before falling into a restless sleep.

At the close of the week, it felt like a year had passed, and Imtiyaaz felt more unsure than ever of his capabilities. He would spend the weekend with his family but from the following week he would need to work weekends too.

Salma had put up a brave front when Imtiyaaz called, but even though she was grateful that Dineo's children lived in the yard, she was afraid at night. The house was in a hilly area and was easy to break into, so she'd barely slept for days. These were all sacrifices that needed to be made. She wouldn't complain.

Imtiyaaz's eyes were bloodshot from exhaustion, but his face was illuminated by a smile. It felt so good to return to his family, even if it was for just two nights. Farzana clung to him, and Salma served him the best food she could, based on what she had.

After they had put Farzana to bed, they sat across each other in their lounge.

"Are you enjoying it?" Salma asked.

"It's different. I am trying. Tough without your cooking!" Imtiyaaz said, breaking into a smile.

"Do you want to get a small fridge in the meantime? Then I can prepare your meals?" she asked.

"Don't worry. I eat at Mr Habib's house. Shortie will stay with me there, but I think Dineo is better off here," Imtiyaaz said.

"Are you learning? What's it like?" Salma asked.

"I do what you said I should. I try to learn from everyone, grassroots level," Imtiyaaz answered.

Salma had provided him with sound advice, and he heard her words ring in his ears at numerous points in his day.

"Do you have enough of everything? Will things last until I get paid?" Imtiyaaz asked.

"They will," Salma assured him.

Salma, who didn't wish to burden him further, did not mention that she had taken detergents and household groceries on credit. She promised to pay within 10 months and, as it was a Muslim-owned shop, there were no interest implications.

The weekend passed slowly and Imtiyaaz cherished every moment. It was more difficult to leave them behind this time as he wouldn't see them save for a Sunday afternoon in two weeks' time.

Mrs Habib passed the potato curry to Imtiyaaz on Wednesday evening.

"You must let me know when you need the van and driver to move your furniture and things," Mr Habib offered.

"I will, thank you," Imtiyaaz said.

"I saw that you stopped Tshepo from stealing the toilet paper rolls. Good job. For months I couldn't understand why we ordered so many packs. Not a failure after all," Mr Habib said. He was a fair man, he offered praise when due and he reprimanded staff when necessary.

"Hotel business is not easy. Do you like it?" Mrs Habib asked.

He thought immediately of Salma. She had asked a similar question. Mrs Habib was active in the business and Imtiyaaz admired how the couple worked as a team, with ever-present respect and trust.

"It's new to me, but I enjoy it. It's great to know that your main function is to service clients... make them happy," Imtiyaaz commented.

"And to make me a profit," Mr Habib joked. "Oh, and I know your daughter needs to go to pre-school, or is it kindergarten? I will help you find a place and pay the deposit if you need," Mr Habib said. His generosity touched Imtiyaaz.

The week dissolved into the weekend and the weekend dissolved into the week. Before Imtiyaaz knew it, it was noon on the Sunday that he could visit his family. He had to see to a guest, though, and there was an issue pertaining to a double booking on the venue hire, so he only managed to leave the hotel at four. He knew he had lost the afternoon and by the time he got home Farzana had already had her evening bath. If Salma was disappointed, she did not show it, and the family enjoyed the few hours that they had together.

"I think it's safe to move," Imtiyaaz said. He told Salma about Mr Habib's offer, and she too was touched.

"Are you sure we shouldn't wait?" Salma asked.

"I think it will be better to move. It's a leap of faith, but it will be easier if we are in one place. Safer too. I cannot leave you here alone. My mind is not at ease," Imtiyaaz said.

And so, the end of the month arrived, and the van moved their furniture, appliances, livestock, and clothing to the company house in three trips. Salma busied herself with cleaning and packing and it felt comforting to be a family again. There were no complaints or any interference. The couple had to be very careful about spending though, as there was much to fix in the home and school fees, despite a deposit paid by the company, was a sizable expense.

Fanta orange and chips became the standard supper and, because they couldn't afford to eat out, they would take it along for a drive.

It was on one such evening that a small voice came from the back seat. "Are we poor?" Farzana asked.

Salma and Imtiyaaz glanced at each other and Imtiyaaz tried to disguise the lump in his throat. "No," he answered.

"We are something called working class. Daddy goes to work to earn money," Salma explained.

The truth was, they were not far from poor, and they made many sacrifices.

Farzana, satisfied with her answer, chewed on her chips. The question haunted both parents as their biggest fear was being unable to give her a decent life.

"Hoosen, tell me something. You came here to the council to report your son?" Patrice asked, his irritation with the man growing.

It was early on Monday morning and Patrice could have thought of a better way to start his day.

"It's a government house. He isn't living in it. He doesn't deserve it," Hoosen moaned.

"Parents die for the well-being of their children. I know Imtiyaaz doesn't live there. He told me himself and he makes his monthly repayments. We made an exception in his case, based on circumstances, and as soon as the repayments are made, he will own that house!" Patrice stated with finality.

Hoosen kicked his chair out from behind the desk at the council office and stormed out. Patrice shook his head in utter disbelief. This man wanted his son to lose even a roof. One that his son paid for. It made no sense.

Imtiyaaz could no longer differentiate between weekends, public holidays and weekdays. The days all transformed into one. Salma joined him on weekends to assist with the workload and for some time Salma's contribution was unpaid. The couple didn't mind at all, though, as the family treated them with kindness despite the demanding nature of the job. Farzana would play and fall off to sleep in Imtiyaaz's office over weekends, but she seemed content.

Five years passed in this fashion, and it was in those years that the business expanded. Imtiyaaz had suggested that they acquire two other buildings on the street and, with a significant amount of work, which Imtiyaaz and Salma managed, the hotel received a 5-star rating, it was featured in international travel magazines, and the restaurant had come to be known for its exquisite cuisine. Weddings, birthdays and corporate events were hosted seamlessly and Imtiyaaz reflected on how he had been intimidated when he had first joined.

"You're here late," Imtiyaaz said looking up from his desk. Mr Habib had walked into his office, unannounced. Imtiyaaz wondered if something was the matter and closed the file he was working on.

"I got carried away, talking to guests," Mr Habib said. "Then I got carried away, thinking about how this business has grown. You have played a phenomenal role; you have made a lot of sacrifices."

"It was all part of the job," Imtiyaaz replied.

Imtiyaaz's humility endeared him to those he worked with, and this was not lost on Mr Habib.

"I want you to take an international trip with your family. You deserve it. Anywhere in the world. All you must do is name it. All expenses paid. I know Farzana is at school now, so I think August is a good time," Mr Habib said.

Imtiyaaz was rather taken aback. He hadn't been on a holiday since his honeymoon. His humility, however, did not leave him. "That's a very generous offer. August is a busy time here and I don't know that I can impose on you like that," Imtiyaaz responded.

"Nonsense! You will go! Boss's orders!" Mr Habib scolded.

A few days later, Mr Habib followed up on whether Imtiyaaz had chosen his preferred destination. Imtiyaaz had, at this stage, not even discussed it with Salma. Imtiyaaz was scolded once more, so he raised the offer with Salma that evening. Salma had just finished making Farzana's school lunch for the next day. It was a sport's day as well, so Salma packed extra treats. Salma placed Farzana at the forefront, and she was always sensitive to her child's needs. She was an outstanding mother who was willing to sacrifice everything of herself for her child.

"That's very generous," Salma said.

She had grown accustomed to them working hard for their living and she wasn't used to anything above and beyond. They were firmly a part of the working class, and she had been reminded of this at a function when a lady who lived two blocks away had done as much as told her she was not welcome company. Salma's heart had been crushed.

Mrs Habib had overheard the comment and had rushed to Salma's side, ensuring that she kept her company the entire night. Salma was embarrassed and where she appreciated Mrs Habib; she knew that Mrs Habib needed to mingle with others. After that, Salma didn't enjoy being invited to functions, but they always seemed to be invited by Mr Habib's extended family and friends.

"I told him it's too generous. He insisted though. Where would you like to go?" he asked Salma.

Imtiyaaz felt that he would like to go to Europe. He longed for his grandmother and Khala and he knew that it would be an opportunity to confront the ill-feelings he had left behind in his aunt's heart. He also wanted to introduce his wife and daughter to Halimah.

"I couldn't decide," Salma confessed.

"Europe? To see my family?" Imtiyaaz suggested.

A sense of knowing engulfed Salma. "It's settled then," Salma said with a reassuring smile.

THE FAMILY DISEMBARKED FROM THE flight and Imtiyaaz's heart rate picked up as they collected their baggage and moved through the airport controls. Aaminah had been rather surprised by the news that Imtiyaaz would be visiting. He had left her out of key occurrences in his life and she hadn't even been aware that he had a daughter until he had said so on the telephone. Aaminah had dropped the glass that she held when his voice had come through the receiver. Aaminah had her misgivings, but she hadn't had the heart to turn him away.

She saw them as soon they passed through the automatic doors. He had married a beautiful lady whose soft curls bounced around her well-defined face and Aaminah felt tears sting her eyes as she saw her sister's grandchild. Imtiyaaz clung to his aunt in an all-encompassing embrace and for those moments Aaminah could have been back in Aguutar with Imtiyaaz as a toddler. Salma warmly introduced herself and Farzana, with excitement in her eyes, clutched the hand of her newly introduced grandmother.

Aaminah had moved into a larger home and Imtiyaaz could not hold himself back. He needed to see his grandmother. He bounded up the stairs and walked through the open front door within seconds of the vehicle stopping outside their home. Imtiyaaz saw her seated in the centre of a three-seater velvet couch. She had on thick-rimmed glasses and wore a floral punjabi. Her hands were wrinkled, and she was hunched.

"Mama," he cried, falling at her feet.

He felt her hand patting his head.

"You came home," came a small voice.

Aaminah, Salma and Farzana appeared in the doorway. Aaminah began to sob openly; her mother had not spoken in such a long time, and it was only her love for Imtiyaaz that elicited vocal communication.

"I am home, Mama, I am home," he responded, kissing her hands.

Salma and Farzana moved to Imtiyaaz's side.

"This is my wife, Salma, and my daughter Farzana," Imtiyaaz said.

"Make me *maaf*, Mama. I am cursed for not having you and Khala as a part of my wedding," Imtiyaaz said, choking on his emotion.

"Our duas are always with you," Halimah replied, in barely a whisper.

Salma began to tear up and Farzana, confused by the situation, followed suit. The family sat in their own emotions for what felt like an hour, and it was only when Aaminah suggested that they freshen up before tea that they met the present.

Imtiyaaz walked into the kitchen after he'd had a shower. Aaminah had put on some tea and was rearranging a platter of freshly fried savouries.

"We wouldn't have imposed at your wedding," Aaminah said bitterly as she looked Imtiyaaz squarely in the eye. Imtiyaaz remained silent. "Do you understand the extent of my mother's sacrifice for you? Or do you not understand how you played with our feelings? What then of when you left us?" Aaminah asked, years' worth of anger ringing through the air. "You think you can come here and that it is all okay? I must wonder what your motive is now!" Aaminah continued, her hands now shaking.

"Khala, I know what everything looks like. I know I hurt you. I couldn't control the wedding plans, and I had no sight of the wedding list. That's not an excuse. I should have demanded to have seen it. You and Mama raised me. My heart beats for Mama," Imtiyaaz began to explain, his voice shaking in a way that matched his aunt's hands.

"I left you last time because I was afraid that, if I stayed, they would have brought you down. I had to do what I did. I was trying to protect you," Imtiyaaz confessed.

"Protect me? Protect me by making me think my only nephew used me? That he felt nothing for me? That he chose someone else over me when I was prepared to risk everything for him?" Aaminah shouted.

"I did what I thought was right," Imtiyaaz explained. He put his head in his hands.

"I don't even know what the truth is anymore," Aaminah said.

"I have left my father. He kicked me out of the business. I work in another city. For another man. He actually paid for my trip here," Imtiyaaz said.

Aaminah's shock was undisguised. He was out of the business?

Imtiyaaz shared the story with his aunt, but she couldn't help wondering if this was a short-lived situation and whether Imtiyaaz was trying to get close to them to spite his father in this spat.

"I know that you cannot forgive me overnight, but this time the truth will prevail. I will give you time and I am willing to spend every living moment proving how much I love you and Mama," Imtiyaaz said.

Aaminah began to tear up again. He was her blood. She had to trust him and all she could do was let him back in. No! No! No! She couldn't. She could not bear abandonment again. She would entertain his visit, but there would be no emotional attachment.

The next three weeks passed with Imtiyaaz spending every waking moment with Halimah, whilst Salma was taken to meet the wider family and do sightseeing. A lot more people had moved from Aguutar. Aaminah was impressed by Salma as Salma was gracious and acted with the utmost consideration for others. Salma was homely and warm, and she was a pleasure to host.

The day that the family was due to leave Imtiyaaz sat at Halimah's side from just after dawn. "I will phone, and I promise to come and see you again. You live in my heart," Imtiyaaz said, clutching onto her the way he had when he was a child.

"Be blessed, my boy," Halimah whispered.

Imtiyaaz wasn't sure if she would live for a next meeting, so he took multiple pictures of her. He needed to remember her. He needed to freeze his moments with her in time.

Imtiyaaz was an emotional wreck as he said his final goodbye after lunch that day. Halimah turned back to her silence as she didn't want to see him leave. Her daughter had a grandchild. How magnificent! Her heart was at peace, despite her not wanting him to leave. Her boy had found a family. She was grateful to have seen it in her lifetime.

Imtiyaaz gazed at his aunt numerous times as they walked back towards the check-in counter. He felt her love, even though she didn't say it.

After they got home, Imtiyaaz kept his word. He called often and he regularly mailed pictures and letters. Halimah would listen to his voice intently on the phone and respond with duas. She was becoming more vocal, and Aaminah noted in amazement the wonderful change in her. This was the power of love.

"WE DID WELL," IMTIYAAZ COMMENTED as he watched his two daughters stand in front of the three-tiered birthday cake.

They were having a birthday dinner on a beach on an exquisite island, known for its pristine beaches and undisturbed marine life.

"We did," Salma agreed, dabbing at her eyes.

Their youngest daughter, Aaliyah, was turning 10. Aaliyah occupied a special place with all three of them as she had faced death as an infant. She had been misdiagnosed with epilepsy by a supposedly renowned doctor who practised at one of the most elite private hospitals in Johannesburg. Salma had wondered if the misdiagnosis was negligent or if her precious child had been used as a guinea pig. Apartheid had just come to an end and Salma had picked up racist traits in the doctor but had hoped that with his expertise he would treat her child.

A nurse had, out of sympathy, approached Salma one night whilst Salma was gazing helplessly at her child in an incubator. She had tipped Salma off about the misdiagnosis and had told her of a new doctor who had just joined the hospital. Imtiyaaz was back at work in a different country so Salma, overcome by both fear and anger, had needed to act swiftly to save her child as she feared that by the time Imtiyaaz came up that weekend Aaliyah would be dead. It was only six weeks later that they were reunited as a happy, healthy family and Salma was continuously grateful to Allah.

It had been a long road, but they had worked through the ranks, and they had also found financial stability, peace and happiness. They had a truly magnificent home, the children had the best that the education system could offer, and the love they had for each other could not be quantified; the latter being the most important.

"I'm really looking forward to Khala's visit next week," Salma said.

They would be back home from their vacation in two days' time and Khala was due to arrive for a visit a few days later.

"Me too," Imtiyaaz said. This would be the third time that they would be hosting her, and it was an absolute joy. Hawa had passed away after a short illness four years ago and Salma had been beside herself. Hawa, had, however passed away with a smile and she had looked to be so much younger. Those who had assisted with the *ghusl* couldn't get over how light her body was and how beautiful she smelt. Hawa had displayed *sabr* until the very end, even when Rashid could no longer work due to heart disease.

Hamza's wife did not approve of him supporting his parents and he had followed her will, despite him being pained for the sake of his own children. He gave where he could, but it was Imtiyaaz who provided a significant amount of money to cover their living expenses. Neither Rashid nor Hawa wished to impose, so when forced to take help they had indicated a lesser amount than what was required, and they'd cut back on a lot.

Imtiyaaz had supported Salma fully during the loss of her mother and he too felt like he had lost a mother. Hawa had been kind and loving towards him and during her sickness she had given him ample duas and asked that he be the one to carry her into her grave. She'd loved him immensely and he had done more than any son-in-law and even more than any son. He had never uttered a word of disrespect.

Salma still missed her mother immensely, but she had now found a new routine and she prayed that they would be reunited in Jannah someday. Salma thought of how her mother had reminded her to always take care of herself as she was always beautiful. Hawa had also instructed her to be happy, no matter what. Salma carried these words with her and, when she closed her eyes, she knew her mom was with her.

Aaliyah flung her arms around Salma and then Imtiyaaz.

"I love you!" she exclaimed. They had spoilt her with multiple gifts and the family dug into their cake, their laughter echoing against the gentle lapping of the waves. This was a memory that would last forever.

Months later, Rashid called on the Mubarak day of *Jumu'a* with the news of Hamza's death.

It was this call that altered their lives. Salma had flung the receiver across her large bedroom, and it had landed on the plush cream carpet whilst she screamed hysterically.

Imtiyaaz, in the shower at the time, rushed out at the sound of his wife's screams.

"Hamza is gone!" she managed to communicate and Imtiyaaz felt the blood drain from his face. Hamza, albeit under the pressure of life, had been an exceptional human being and Imtiyaaz loved him as a brother. Memories came down upon Imtiyaaz and for once he could offer no support. He floated to an armchair in the lounge, still in his bathrobe, and sat motionless. Hamza. Hamza was dead. Imtiyaaz's sense of reason returned slowly, and he went into denial. He called

Saida and when she tearfully confirmed, Imtiyaaz demanded to know what had happened.

"It seems like a heart attack," Saida said before collapsing into tears.

Flight arrangements were made, and Hamza was laid in his grave after *Asr.*

"We lost," Rashid said to his granddaughter.

"We did," she responded, as she tried to seek comfort from her inconsolable grandfather. It was unnatural to lose a child and Rashid thought of how Hamza had survived an illness in his childhood. He heard his voice and saw his smile. Rashid knew that he would not heal.

Salma returned home a week after Imtiyaaz and for the next month they travelled up for the weekends. Salma was rather surprised that, on their first weekend home, Imtiyaaz mentioned that they would be having guests over for lunch. She was even more surprised to hear that it was Hoosen and Zohra! They had attended Hamza's funeral, but Salma had not interacted much with them in her state, and, prior to that, she had last spoken to Zohra on a call after Hawa's death. Zohra had called to let her know that it was an embarrassment that Rashid was unable to provide for Hawa's own funeral (even though every grain of rice used had come from Rashid and Hawa's home). She had made sure that she reminded Salma of her poverty-stricken background and Salma had said nothing until Zohra put the phone down.

"Why are they coming over?" Salma asked, confused.

"I made peace. Life is short. Your brother's death taught me that," Imtiyaaz said.

Salma felt the room spin. Imtiyaaz had the right to forgive and bring them into their home, but things had not ended well, and their actions had had a huge impact on Salma's life as well.

They arrived at noon and Salma, despite her misgivings, welcomed them into their home. Zohra and Hoosen could not believe what they saw. Imtiyaaz had reached a level of success that they had not anticipated, and Zohra felt her insides burn. If she could have torn down the walls, she would have. How was this even possible? She thought she had destroyed them.

Salma felt uneasy, but Imtiyaaz, in an almost bizarre trance, shared intimate details of his status and showed them around the house and grounds. They left before *maghrib*, and Salma finally snapped.

"These were the same people who threw you out on the road! Forgive them. Fine! But to share financial details? Why would you do that? I walked this road with you, and it wasn't easy. The least you could have done was protect our privacy," Salma said.

Imtiyaaz did not answer and for every Sunday thereafter Hoosen and Zohra came over for lunch.

It was a Tuesday evening in October when Imtiyaaz announced that he didn't wish to continue with life the way it was. He wanted to live in Johannesburg, as the girls were growing up and needed to further their studies.

Salma, who hadn't anticipated this, asked him for solid reasoning, as they had built their lives here and the children could study overseas or wherever they were given the opportunity without the family moving. Imtiyaaz withdrew into silence and Salma found him shaking uncontrollably the next day. He was seated in his favourite armchair. Salma, in a complete panic, immediately sought medical help.

Their family doctor arrived at their house. He diagnosed Imtiyaaz with anxiety and administered an injection to settle Imtiyaaz. It seemed to have worked and Salma closed the bedroom door so that Imtiyaaz could rest. Aaliyah needed to be fetched from school and Salma liked doing this herself. Today would have been an exception as she was worried about Imtiyaaz, but it was a bit too late to make alternative pick-up arrangements. She instructed the help to watch over Imtiyaaz and she sped towards school. She tried to put on a face of normalcy, and she informed Aaliyah that Daddy wouldn't be having lunch with them today as he wasn't well. Salma barely ate but, in order to maintain things, she sat at the table with Aaliyah. It was only when Aaliyah was at madressah that Salma heard the bedroom door open.

Imtiyaaz drew a picture of a clock on their exquisite, tiled floor. "By 6 I will be dead," he said in a firm voice.

Fear gripped Salma.

"Imtiyaaz! What are you saying?" she yelled. He began to tremble once more, and Salma called the doctor again. Two days later he was diagnosed as having had a nervous breakdown. All responsibility came crashing down on Salma and, what was worse, this needed to be concealed from the children.

THE PHONE RINGING INTERRUPTED SALMA'S troubled thoughts early on a Thursday morning.

"I've been thinking about it. It's not possible that you have accumulated so much. Imtiyaaz must have stolen from us and other people!" came Zohra's voice.

Salma felt the fury rise. They had worked day and night and earned their position! Blood, sweat, tears and then some more tears. An honest living was critical to both her and Imtiyaaz and they had never strayed. Salma didn't have the energy for Zohra's antics, especially now with Imtiyaaz's medical condition. Salma remained silent and it was only after a few minutes of silence that Zohra ended the call. They didn't come over that weekend and Salma was beyond grateful.

FOR EIGHT MONTHS SALMA ASSUMED all responsibilities. If it wasn't enough that she had to watch over Imtiyaaz for fear that he may hurt himself; she had to seamlessly orchestrate the move to Johannesburg. They did have a property purchased, which was intended to be used as a holiday home, so that did lessen the load to an extent. The question of "why the move" haunted Salma but, under the pressure that Imtiyaaz piled on with suicide threats, Salma had given in. She found herself packing up not only items but beautiful memories. The house would not be sold, so furniture and curtains remained intact, but Salma knew that things would never be the same.

Tears filled her eyes on the day that they closed the door to their home for the final time. She recalled the day they had moved in. She thought of the hours spent in the garden on summer afternoons, and she remembered the evenings that they had hosted family and friends. This house represented so much, and it was not a place that could easily be forgotten. She had to bid farewell to some staff members who would not be joining them, and this broke her heart. She had tried to assist in securing them employment but had not been successful in all her attempts with some of the domestic staff.

She drove their vehicle up on that dreadful day whilst Imtiyaaz trembled in the seat next to her. For days, Salma tried to settle into their new house, but she found herself lost and anxious.

With time and under all the emotional trauma, Salma found that it did help to be around Saida, to the exclusion of Saida's husband, and Saida dutifully visited and tried to assist where she could. Rashid too ensured that he visited often and provided support.

A few months into the move, Salma assessed the situation. There had been no improvement in Imtiyaaz. Salma decided that the medical intervention was not assisting, and she noted the impact on herself and the children. So, for the first time she wondered if paranormal activity could be at play. Salma was frightened by the thought, and she had not confronted a similar situation before. She reached out to Bonny's eldest son, as they had a wonderful family relationship, and Salma voiced her pertinent concerns.

In the matter of a few days, they had arranged for Imtiyaaz to be seen to. She communicated this to Imtiyaaz who had simply stared at her. That evening, he had tried to locate car keys as he had resolved to drive his car off the highway. It was Salma who had found him digging through drawers and, in a trance-like state, he had made his plan known. He had a fierce strength but, with the domestic help who had come with them to Johannesburg, they had managed to settle him. Salma did not leave Imtiyaaz unattended thereafter and all items that could pose a threat were taken out of reach.

The day of the consultation finally arrived, and Salma planned to get him there without any hurdles. Imtiyaaz was placed under treatment immediately and Salma was tasked with overseeing that all steps were followed. The next few weeks were arguably more difficult than the months that had passed, but eventually Imtiyaaz returned to a state where he could reason, where the trembling stopped, and where he was able to take stock of what had occurred.

Aaliyah had been enrolled into a new school by this stage and, despite the school being prestigious with multiple facilities offered, Aaliyah struggled to adjust. The move had been too abrupt and, where she had excelled and enjoyed every day at her previous school, she struggled at this one. Aaliyah was unable to break into friendship circles and befriended two other loners. This did nothing for her self-esteem and she was subjected to being bullied via association. Her grades began to slip. She had been an A-student with the quality of her work internationally recognised, but she could not cope with the emotional trauma at home as well as the adjustment to a new life in a new country under very different circumstances.

Aaliyah feared for her father's life constantly, even though he had now recovered, and she would find herself raising her hands in prayer for his safety multiple times a day. This became an obsession, and she would go and make dua for him every few minutes. There is no harm in dua, if anything, her reliance on Allah as the Only One who could Assist was built, but she had a paralysing fear that her father would slip back into the breakdown.

Imtiyaaz had, however, now healed and he continued to be an outstanding being with a contagious smile and warm heart. It remained unclear to both Salma and Imtiyaaz whether he had in fact gone through a nervous breakdown in medical terms or whether he had been a victim of dark forces. This shall be Revealed on the Day of Reckoning.

Aaliyah's unhappiness was noted by her parents, and they briefly considered moving back, but this was shelved as they now had a new life. Imtiyaaz settled into business and life began to reach some level of normalcy. Imtiyaaz maintained strong links of contact with his father and Zohra and, while she feared having them involved in their lives, Salma remained silent. She eventually accepted the situation for what it was, and she put on a smiling face when forced to interact. Imtiyaaz was happy with the arrangement and, as he was healthy, Salma eventually placed her fears aside.

THE HOUSE WAS ABUZZ WITH wedding preparations. Salma, the ever-gracious host, paid very little attention to her own feelings about Farzana's upcoming nuptials as she tended to entertaining guests over a two-week period. Khala had arrived and this had, despite the couple's reservations about the wedding, brought great joy to both Salma and Imtiyaaz as she stood in as a mother for them.

Farzana had met the young man at university as they were both studying towards the same degree. Farzana, however, had been selected to complete her Honours and he had not, so he had taken up employment in his father's business until he could find a role as a professional. As they were in their very early twenties and he was not financially stable, Farzana had agreed to live with her in-laws. They had a family of five and Farzana, having lived away from home in the past, was ready to embrace her new life even though she knew that it would not be at the level of comfort that she had at home.

Imtiyaaz and Salma harboured concerns about his lack of independence but they gave in to Farzana's will. Salma's concerns had not dissipated, even with the wedding fast approaching, but she distracted herself with the functions. Imtiyaaz made a concerted effort to bond with the other family and had set up dinners and allowed him to visit their home occasionally. He too, however, could not shake a feeling of being unsettled but he eventually put it down to anxiety about giving his eldest daughter away.

Each function was well-planned and Zohra and Hoosen had not missed a meal. Salma, at this stage, knew that they did it for the free entertainment and to ensure that they maintained a good name in Johannesburg. The trustees watched closely and concluded that Hoosen had made a great decision to let Imtiyaaz go out on his own. They had built a life and now had mutual respect. The trustees decided that on

Imtiyaaz's fiftieth birthday, which was four years away, they would pass on some of his share. Hoosen couldn't have much to say about it. They had obviously ironed out their differences.

What wasn't noted by them was Zohra's envy.

The day of the wedding arrived and, before Salma knew it, she was welcoming guests into the venue. The function resembled something out of a fairy-tale and Salma and Imtiyaaz put the reddish hue of the groom's eyes down to exhaustion. Before midnight, the couple left to begin their lives in his family home. It was there that Farzana juggled between her studies, attending to chores, and staying up all night for fear of being harmed. Her husband, suffered from a condition of sorts under which he grew violent, but had no memory of it. Farzana hid this horrible truth, but it was Salma who noted that Farzana's hair was unkempt, that her eyes were sunken, and that her once glowing smile had been replaced with a pasted-on one.

After some cajoling, Farzana shared the truth but begged Salma to remain silent as she had the matter under control and wanted to make her marriage a success. Salma upheld her daughter's wish, against her own better judgement, and this began to take a toll on her health.

Imtiyaaz saw that his pillar was being slowly chipped away, and he grew concerned and implored Salma to share with him her concerns. Salma resisted until she could no longer and, when she saw the fury assume control of Imtiyaaz, she wondered for a moment if she had made the wrong decision. Imtiyaaz and Salma had cared for their children too much for them to meet a fate like this. Salma had to restrain Imtiyaaz from going to the house that night and she assured him that Farzana now knew how to protect herself, even if it meant that she slept with one eye open. This was what Farzana had convinced Salma of at least. Salma also feared for her daughter's life, but Farzana had been quite brazen in her attempts to save the marriage.

It was before 10 the next morning that Imtiyaaz arrived at Farzana's home, and she knew from the moment he entered that he was aware of the truth. Farzana returned home with him on that day, and this would be the beginning of a conflict within a home that was usually characterised by love. Farzana feared the stigma of divorce. She considered the impact that a divorce would have on her family's reputation and the future of her little sister, and she was concerned that she would never be loved again. The idea of loneliness depressed her. No one ever marries to seek divorce.

Imtiyaaz and Salma's attempts to help Farzana see beyond her fears were futile and Farzana chose to return to her marriage. Imtiyaaz had reached a point of no return. He loved his child endlessly and could not bear to think that her life was at risk, that he was helpless to protect her, and that she had condemned herself to an unsafe and unhappy life.

Salma's sleep was lost, and her heart ached for what her child was experiencing.

Imtiyaaz put in an ultimatum to the effect that, if she wished to live in that marriage, she would no longer be welcome in his home. It was two weeks later that Farzana returned home and the next challenge faced was to obtain the divorce. This was finally given, and Farzana began her process of healing, a process that would be rushed along by a trauma yet to come.

SALMA TURNED THE PAGES OF her recipe book and smiled when she found the page she was looking for. Imtiyaaz loved this recipe, and he had said that he would finish earlier today as he wanted to go shopping and, of course, to buy treats for the upcoming Ramadaan. She loved to bake and, as she had to be home today because of minor renovations taking place, she opted to use the time for that.

Imtiyaaz closed his office door and hesitated for a moment. He walked away from the door slowly, leaving it unlocked. He gazed at the greenery around him before walking towards his black car, parked outside the building.

"Laaillaha illallahu muhammdur rasulullah" (I bear witness that there is None Worthy of Worship Besides Allah and that Muhammed is His Final Messenger) Imtiyaaz said thrice as he laid himself on the ground. A smile decorated his face, despite the pool of blood emanating

from the bullet. A shot had been fired by a man stationed behind him and Imtiyaaz had realised with utmost clarity that it was time for him to leave the world. His eyes closed and his last thought went to his family.

Salma turned off her Kenwood to answer the phone.

"Ma'am," came a shaky voice, "the boss is shot. Just the boss."

Salma recognised the employee's voice, and she began to scream. The entire household, workmen included, followed her shrill cries to the kitchen. "Imtiyaaz! He is shot!" she yelled, her tears pouring onto the floor in the way in which his blood had.

Saida, who had a shop near the business, had been informed of the shooting and had rushed to the site. Saida knew instantly that there was no need for the paramedics who had gathered. Imtiyaaz was gone.

The hours that passed thereafter were a blur, and it felt surreal to be sitting next to Imtiyaaz's body with their two children. Salma thought of the life they had shared and the unbreakable commitment they had made to each other. Her mind took her to their twenty-fifth wedding anniversary, which had taken place three weeks ago, on which she had bounded down the staircase to tell him that they'd made it 25 years and that she was looking forward to the next 25.

He had smiled but remained silent. He had gifted her a beautiful bracelet and in the days after that he had been in a flurry to purchase her make-up and clothes. He had also purchased multiple items for the children and Aaliyah had just received a new mobile. She thought of Shaab-e-Baraat, where he had been glowing in a way likened to the moon, and she thought of how she had heard him practising the questions of the grave a few days ago. She had asked him about it, and he had told her that she had been full of questions of late.

Salma came to the heart-breaking conclusion that he had known that his time had come, as most people do when death beckons, and that he had taken steps to provide him with comfort; like purchasing items for his family, as he knew that they wouldn't have the heart for it in the months and perhaps years that followed. She remembered how he had sat her down the previous week to discuss their full financial position and how he had asked her to always respect his father, no matter what.

Hoosen had arrived at their house without Zohra when he heard of the shooting and a few tears had fallen. The funeral arrangements, however, were handled by other family members and neighbours. Imtiyaaz was well-loved and this showed by the people who had travelled from far and wide to attend his funeral.

Salma's mind then went to their children. Aaliyah was only 14 and would now be growing up without her father. Farzana and Aaliyah were inconsolable, and Aaliyah blamed herself for being unable to assist and protect her father, despite her premonition that he was in danger. The *mayyit* was lifted after Esha, a week before Ramadaan set in, and Imtiyaaz was laid to rest under a tree. People spoke endlessly about his smile, his warm nature, his generosity and how much he loved his family.

All but Zohra. They were seated in the dining room a few days after his passing and Zohra had clearly stated that she wouldn't want her children to die the way Imtiyaaz did. Salma heard her words but held her tongue. Imtiyaaz had passed away a martyr. The family was now in shreds, and each wondered how they would face life without him as their shelter, so they paid little consideration to Zohra's words.

Salma had lost her sense of taste. Her heart was shattered, and her mind was ablaze with thoughts of who would want her husband dead. The investigating officer had brought her photographs of the scene, and they had discussed witnesses. The photographs had tormented her, and she did not wish to remember him in any way other than the way they had parted, with the words, "Allah Take Care of you."

Salma had been advised against pursuing the murder case as whoever it was may take revenge. She trusted the advice from her close family and advisor. She had been told that there was a difference between the cause of the death and coping with the death itself and she knew that, for the sake of her children, she needed to pull herself together so that they could deal with their grief as a family.

Salma's mind, however, constantly took her to whether his inheritance could have been the cause, or whether someone in business had wanted him out of the way. It didn't strike her as anything related to a robbery, as nothing was stolen from him, except his life. She then had the worry about the restructuring of finances for the next few months, until the estate had settled and until they found their feet. Private school fees were exorbitantly expensive, and Salma had felt a weight taken off her shoulders when she had received a letter from the school indicating that they would waive the first two terms of fees.

There were, however, still tough financial constraints and Salma had to make some decisions. Farzana had long put aside her pain over the divorce, as this was a bigger ordeal. It had been ordained for both mother and daughter to serve their *Iddah* period in the same year.

Salma looked at Aaliyah's innocence one Thursday afternoon as she lay sprawled across the bed. She would shower to sleep and sleep to shower, with very little effort thrown into anything else. Her depression was clear and, even though the school had made available to her the services of a psychologist, she had drifted to a distant, dark place of solitude and pain.

"Farzana," Salma called.

"Jee, Mom," Farzana answered, rising from her place.

"I need to ask you something. It is something huge. I am left as a single parent. Your sister is still young and will feel the gap of Dad's death. Please help me love her. Please help me to try and close that gap," Salma said, her voice catching in her sobs.

Farzana joined her mother in tears as they watched Aaliyah sleep. "I promise," Farzana said, clasping her mother's hand.

The months to come were perhaps the most difficult experienced but, despite what happened behind closed doors, Salma put on a brave face. She encouraged Farzana to do the same and she knew that her encouragement was lost on Aaliyah. Months passed in which they ate in the lounge as they could not bear the realisation that the table, set for four out of habit, would only be filled by three.

Saida and Rashid, understanding that things were still being sorted financially, assisted with purchasing necessities, and Salma was filled with gratitude. It was remarkable how the grandfather who didn't have much cared for his grandchildren, but the one who dwelled in luxury contributed nothing.

Zohra had informed Salma that they would not be coming to their home any longer and Salma had not realised the gravity of what was said until 15 years had passed. In those fifteen years, Zohra and Hoosen had gone about their lives, travelled and fully enjoyed their time, whilst Salma had invested her whole self for the well-being of her children. Hoosen did not bother to check on whether they lived or not, and he had once met Farzana outside a shop and, noting that she had a new car, he had asked her about how her car was as opposed to how her mom and sister were. This was who he was – the one who, despite his prayers, disregarded his responsibility to his grandchildren.

It is, however, Allah Who Will Decide the outcome. Salma and her children often sought the answers to who had taken their beloved away but then came the realisation that he was never theirs to begin with. He Belonged to Allah, as they did, and it was now a question of living life until they could meet again and be a family for eternity.

A time came when Aaliyah and Salma had wept in their loneliness, when Farzana remarried and moved away. It was months before they established a new routine in their lives. They reached normality eventually, and Aaliyah seemed to have found a reason to live. Aaliyah had risen after she had fallen and they had worked together, as a unit, to find the butterflies of hope, even in the most trying times. It had not been easy, and hearts had been mended just to break again, but 15 years later they stood at Hoosen's death bed.

Aaliyah watched as her aunt fed her grandfather with a spoon. He was in a ward at a private hospital, about ten minutes from their home, but the drive there had felt like it had taken hours to conclude. Aaliyah wasn't sure if she pitied him or not, and she had noted quite acutely that her father's youngest brother had completely disregarded her and Salma.

Salma chatted amicably and, despite everything, she was disheartened at his condition. Aaliyah and Salma retreated to the reception area and Salma insisted that they stay a few minutes longer to support the family. Aaliyah reluctantly obliged, but she was fully aware of the coldness.

Hoosen's condition gradually worsened over the next month, and he was in and out of hospital. Salma visited him on a Monday evening.

"Water please, Salma," he murmured.

Salma immediately stood up and approached a nurse. "Am I able to give my father-in-law some water?" she asked.

"No, he cannot have any. He brings it up," the nurse cautioned.

"What else can I do for him?" Salma asked.

"I am afraid, very little," the nurse responded. The nurse turned away and pretended to busy herself with a file.

Salma stepped back towards his bed and patted his hand. She tried to explain to him why he couldn't have water, and she apologised. He did not respond and slipped into a state of unconsciousness.

It was before mid-morning the next day that he passed. Salma had been the last person that he had sought help from. Salma forgave him for his actions and his omissions, and she hoped that her children would do the same.

The girls arrived at the funeral later than Salma and they were ushered into the *mayyit* room. Aaliyah and Farzana, who sat side by side, with Farzana's two precious kids, prayed for the man they knew as nothing else but a biological grandfather. Aaliyah wept, not for him, but for what could have been had he just shown them love or acknowledgement.

Zohra fainted during the funeral, and it was Salma who rushed to her aid. This was the beginning of a very serious illness. It would be only another three weeks before they were gathered in the reception area of the hospital; this time for an ill Zohra.

"Things don't look good," Safiyyah, who was one of Imtiyaaz's siblings, said.

"Just hope for the best," Salma responded.

"We are looking into the estate. Things will be divided amongst the living siblings," Safiyyah said, eyeing Salma and Farzana.

Farzana didn't hold her tongue. "We are not here to discuss the estate. We came to show our support. No obligations towards us were ever fulfilled by any of you. It doesn't matter that we will be excluded from the estate. We survived without it," she said.

Salma watched Farzana in horror, but she understood the context. It had taken a lot out of Farzana to even come to the hospital to see Zohra. This was uncalled for.

Safiyyah did not answer.

"Mom, they got away with it," Aaliyah commented later that evening. Aaliyah was lying on the couch, massaging her temples.

"Don't worry about it. I know Dad gave a lot. He was abused, and he was pulled out of school. Torment after torment. So, it will hurt that he didn't get what was rightfully his, but this isn't the ultimate," Salma assured her.

"I know that, Mom. That's why Farzana said to Safiyyah what she said. It's just unfair. That's all. I couldn't care less, even if they took our right, but it just amazes me that Zohra got what she wanted," Aaliyah said, with a deep sigh.

"Things will work out for the best. Let's be grateful that Allah Took Care of us," Salma said to her daughter.

"I just look at fairness," Aaliyah replied.

Salma knew her daughter had an innate sense of what is moral and correct and that it was easy for her to get stuck in that. The thing was that the world worked in a very different way, where one couldn't expect from others the same level of morality as one possessed.

The news of Zohra's critical condition came a few weeks later and, once more, Salma stepped in to support the family. She thought of all that she had been subjected to by Zohra and her children but, as she stood at Zohra's bedside, in the way that she had with Hoosen, Salma forgave her. It was not for Salma to hold on to a dirty heart. She was beyond that, a human from a different class.

"Khala, she passed away," Salma said late one evening.

"Jee, my child," Aaminah answered, cradling the telephone. Aaminah thought of her sister Khadeejah and how she had left the world so many years before Hoosen and Zohra. She thought of the torment that she couldn't stop, and she saw now that life was not guaranteed. Zohra may have lived well at the expense of Imtiyaaz, but she too had tasted death. She too hadn't lived to deplete all the funds. She too had returned to her Maker.

EPILOGUE - BAMBA BUTTERFLY

The ease of an ending cannot be linked to the difficulty of a beginning nor to the mountains climbed or descended during life. It is for us to ensure that hope is kept alive, that forgiveness is kept at the forefront, and that the Will of the Almighty is fully accepted and followed. Our hearts should be directed only at the end, for it is the end that determines Eternity. It is Allah Who has the capability to Forgive even the gravest sinner, and it cannot be for us to pass judgement, even from a place of oppression. There are butterflies of hope that surround all of us, but should we someday seek them and note their absence, we should then strive to become one of them for the benefit of ourselves and those around us.